MODERN WORLD

CULTURES

Africa South of the Sahara

◆

Australia and the Pacific

◆

East Asia

◆

Europe

◆

Latin America

◆

North Africa and the Middle East

◆

Northern America

◆

Russia and
the Former Soviet Republics

◆

South Asia

◆

Southeast Asia

◆

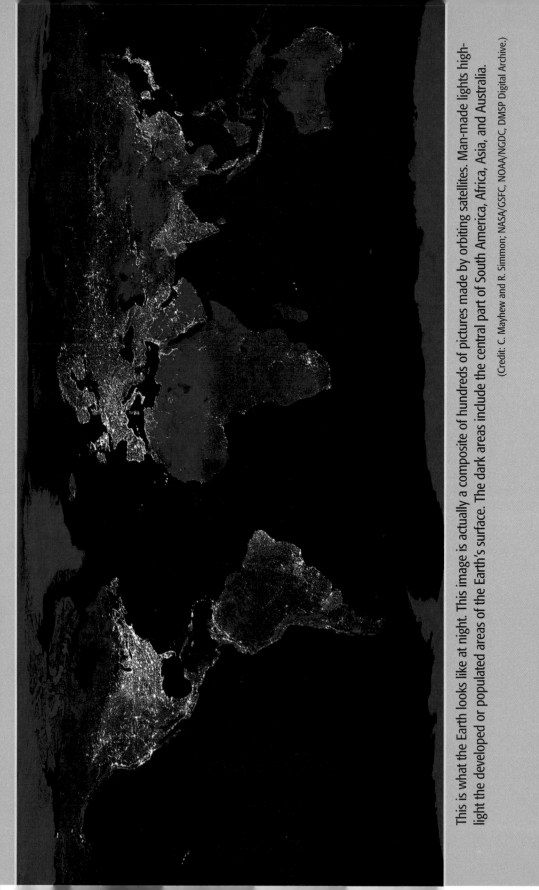

This is what the Earth looks like at night. This image is actually a composite of hundreds of pictures made by orbiting satellites. Man-made lights highlight the developed or populated areas of the Earth's surface. The dark areas include the central part of South America, Africa, Asia, and Australia.

(Credit: C. Mayhew and R. Simmon; NASA/GSFC, NOAA/NGDC, DMSP Digital Archive.)

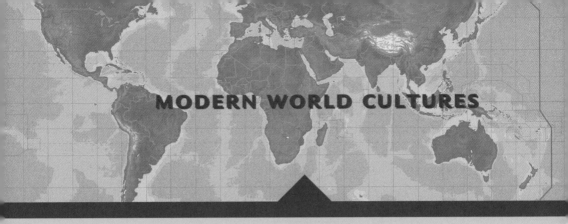

MODERN WORLD CULTURES

East Asia

Douglas A. Phillips

Senior Consultant
Center for Civic Education
Calabasas, CA

Series Consulting Editor
Charles F. Gritzner
South Dakota State University

CHELSEA HOUSE
PUBLISHERS
A Haights Cross Communications Company ®
Philadelphia

This book is dedicated to my wife, Marlene Phillips. Our journey in life has allowed me the privilege of traveling together with her over the years and distances that have taken us from South Dakota, to Alaska, and now to our home in Arizona. Her strength in the face of adverse health is an inspiration to all who know her and especially to me.

Cover: Workers tending to the tea crop in Hangzhou, China

CHELSEA HOUSE PUBLISHERS

VP, NEW PRODUCT DEVELOPMENT Sally Cheney
DIRECTOR OF PRODUCTION Kim Shinners
CREATIVE MANAGER Takeshi Takahashi
MANUFACTURING MANAGER Diann Grasse
PRODUCTION EDITOR Noelle Nardone
PHOTO EDITOR Sarah Bloom

Staff for GLOBALIZATION, LANGUAGE, AND CULTURE

EDITOR Lee M. Marcott
EDITORIAL ASSISTANT Joseph Gialanella
DEVELOPMENTAL EDITOR Carol Field
PROJECT MANAGER Michael Henry
SERIES AND COVER DESIGNER Takeshi Takahashi
LAYOUT Maryland Composition Company, Inc.

A Haights Cross Communications Company ®

www.chelseahouse.com

First Printing

10 9 8 7 6 5 4 3 2 1

Library of Congress Cataloging-in-Publication Data

Phillips, Douglas A.
East Asia / Douglas A. Phillips.
p. cm.—(Modern world cultures)
Audience: Grades 9-12.
ISBN 0-7910-8148-6 (hard cover)
1. East Asia—Juvenile literature. I. Title. II. Series.
DS504.5.P47 2005

2005010041

TABLE OF CONTENTS

	Introduction	vi
1	Introducing East Asia	1
2	Natural Environment	7
3	East Asia's Past	19
4	A Century of Transition and Change	41
5	The People of East Asia	55
6	Governments in East Asia	71
7	East Asian Economics	88
8	East Asia Looks Ahead	104
	History at a Glance	109
	Bibliography	113
	Further Reading	115
	Index	118

Charles F. Gritzner

Geography is the key that unlocks the door to the world's wonders. There are, of course, many ways of viewing the world and its diverse physical and human features. In this series—MODERN WORLD CULTURES—the emphasis is on people and their cultures. As you step through the geographic door into the ten world cultures covered in this series, you will come to better know, understand, and appreciate the world's mosaic of peoples and how they live. You will see how different peoples adapt to, use, and change their natural environments. And you will be amazed at the vast differences in thinking, doing, and living practiced around the world. The MODERN WORLD CULTURES series was developed in response to many requests from librarians and teachers throughout the United States and Canada.

As you begin your reading tour of the world's major cultures, it is important that you understand three terms that are used throughout the series: geography, culture, and region. These words and their meanings are often misunderstood. **Geography** is an age-old way of viewing the varied features of Earth's surface. In fact, it is the oldest of the existing sciences! People have always had a need to know about and understand their surroundings. In times past, a people's world was their immediate surroundings; today, our world is global in scope. Events occuring half a world away can and often do have an immediate impact on our lives. If we, either individually or as a nation of peoples, are to be successful in the global community, it is essential that we know and understand our neighbors, regardless of who they are or where they may live.

Geography and history are similar in many ways; both are method-ologies—distinct ways of viewing things and events. Historians are concerned with time, or when events happened. Geographers, on the other hand, are concerned with space, or where things are located. In essence, geographers ask: "What is where, why there, and why care?" in regard to various physical and human features of Earth's surface.

Culture has many definitions. For this series and for most geogra-phers and anthropologists, it refers to a people's way of life. This means the totality of everything we possess because we are human, such as our ideas, beliefs, and customs, including language, religious beliefs, and all knowledge. Tools and skills also are an important aspect of culture. Dif-ferent cultures, after all, have different types of technology and levels of technological attainment that they can use in performing various tasks. Finally, culture includes social interactions—the ways different people interact with one another individually and as groups.

Finally, the idea of **region** is one geographers use to organize and ana-lyze geographic information spatially. A region is an area that is set apart from others on the basis of one or more unifying elements. Language, reli-gion, and major types of economic activity are traits that often are used by geographers to separate one region from another. Most geographers, for example, see a cultural division between Northern, or Anglo, America and Latin America. That "line" is usually drawn at the U.S.–Mexico boundary, although there is a broad area of transition and no actual cultural line exists.

The ten culture regions presented in this series have been selected on the basis of their individuality, or uniqueness. As you tour the world's culture realms, you will learn something of their natural environment, history, and way of living. You will also learn about their population and settlement, how they govern themselves, and how they make their living. Finally, you will take a peek into the future in the hope of identifying each region's challenges and prospects. Enjoy your trip! ◼

Charles F. ("Fritz") Gritzner
Department of Geography
South Dakota State University
May 2005

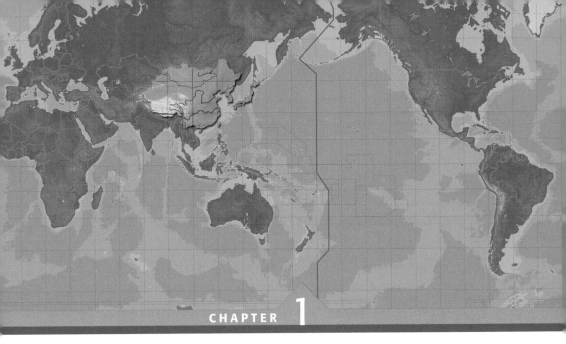

CHAPTER 1

Introducing East Asia

The term *East Asia* brings to mind countries filled with people in crowded cities bustling about their daily business. This is true of some of the region, but there is also a huge agricultural sector in countries such as the People's Republic of China (PRC). The PRC is the world's most populous nation, with nearly 1.3 billion people! Mongolia, in contrast, is one of the world's most sparsely populated lands. The world's second- and third-largest economies are in East Asia, but one country, North Korea, is unable to adequately feed its people. These and many other striking contrasts exist in this complex and fascinating region. This region is thousands of years old, its past richly filled with intrusions, intrigue, inventions, and interplay.

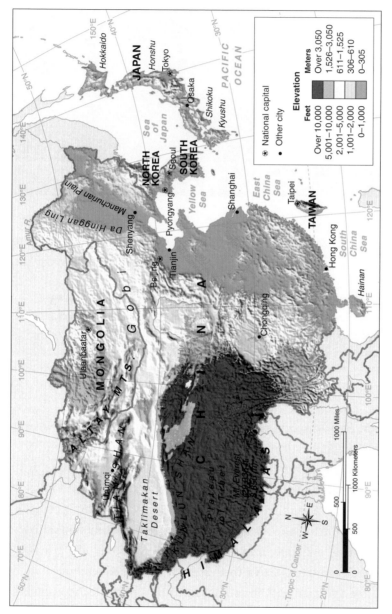

This reference map of East Asia shows the countries, cities, and major landforms of the region. With the exception of Mongolia, all of these countries lie on the Pacific Ocean.

This is a view from the Li River, China. Visitors from around the world come to take the leisurely five-hour river cruise that passes through hundreds of beautiful limestone formations along the river's banks.

East Asia includes mainland China, Mongolia, North Korea, South Korea, Taiwan, and Japan. All except Taiwan are recognized countries with seats in the United Nations and other major international bodies. Taiwan is unique in that the People's Republic of China (PRC or China) considers the island to be its renegade twenty-third province. Thus, Taiwan's international relations differ from those of the other countries in the region. It is not technically a country, although it operates independently of mainland China.

The Li River gently flows through the Guangxi Zhuang Autonomous Region in China. Visitors from around the world come to take the leisurely five-hour river cruise that passes through hundreds of beautiful limestone formations along the river's banks. Here, cormorants are used to catch fish. Fishermen can be seen loosening the nooses on the birds' necks so that they can breathe but cannot swallow the fish that they dive to catch! Fish are extracted from the birds' beaks, and then the hungry birds are sent back to fish again. Every bend of the river brings a new vista, and the clouds that top the limestone formations create an atmosphere of mystery. Fishing villages along the river reveal a life that started long ago; many traditions of this life are still maintained.

Today, East Asia has become an economic powerhouse. China, Japan, South Korea, and Taiwan are major players on the world's economic stage. North Korea stands in sharp contrast to these economic giants. This country lies dormant as a political exile from most of the world because of its repressive Communist government. Mongolia is also different because it is landlocked. Goods that enter or leave the country must pass through China or Russia, its two neighboring countries. Today, the country hopes to regain some of the strength that it had in the past.

East Asia is a huge region, and it holds nearly one-fourth of the world's population. It is bordered to the north by the world's largest country, sprawling Russia. To the east, it is bordered by the Pacific Ocean and extends to include the Korean Peninsula and the islands of Japan and Taiwan. The southern border is formed by boundaries with the Vietnam, Laos, Burma (Myanmar), and Bhutan. To the southwest are India and Nepal. Pakistan, Afghanistan, Tajikistan, and Kyrgyzstan are located to the west. Kazakhstan borders East Asia on the northwest. China itself, the world's fourth-largest country, shares its border with 14 nations! This does not include others nearby via the sea such as Japan, South Korea, and Taiwan— although the Chinese maintain that Taiwan is part of China.

Much of the region is subject to natural hazards. Devastating earthquakes have killed hundreds of thousands of people and have caused billions of dollars in damage to property. Much of the land that borders or lies within the Pacific Ocean is in the path of typhoons (hurricane-like storms) that can strike with vicious winds and drenching rain.

Flooding is common in many areas, and withering drought is in others. East Asia experiences extremely diverse environmental conditions. To the south, it is bordered by the Himalayas, the world's highest mountain range, whereas eastern China has vast areas of fertile plains. The region's climates and ecosystems include areas that are hot, humid, and forested; parched deserts; and frigid lands buried beneath fields of ice and snow.

With the exception of Mongolia, all countries lie on the Pacific Ocean, which gives these lands valuable access to international trade. Vital resources such as petroleum and natural gas can be brought into the region, and manufactured goods can be exported to other countries at low cost. Historically, the Pacific served as a protective barrier from outsiders, but today the ocean serves as an important linkage.

With a history that spans thousands of years, East Asia easily could get trapped in its romantic past. Japan, South Korea, China, and Taiwan are vibrant modern societies, however, with very productive economies. The rise of democratic governments in Taiwan, South Korea, Japan, and Mongolia in the second half of the twentieth century has provided for greater citizen involvement in political processes. China and North Korea remain trapped in Communist regimes, but China has made rapid advances. In terms of manufacturing and technology, the country has one of the fastest economic growth rates in the world. In 2003, China became the third country to successfully orbit an astronaut around the earth.

Japan, Taiwan, and South Korea are known for their cutting-edge technology. In fact, East Asia increasingly competes successfully with the United States and Western Europe for advances in science and research. The results of this research have allowed the region to become a leader in medicine, transportation, communication, and entertainment. Companies like Sony, Samsung, Toyota, Nissan, Panasonic, Nintendo, Sega, Goldstar, Haier, and Pioneer market excellent products that are sold around the world.

Some problems exist in the region: China, for example, suffers from air and water pollution, deforestation, acid rain, and severe erosion. Many endangered species of animals are hunted to appease the Chinese appetite for exotic foods and medicine. At the same time, North Korea is unable to feed its own people, and hunger and malnutrition plague the country. In addition, North Korea faces environmental problems. Most of Japan's environmental issues are associated with urbanization. The country is plagued with problems such as air pollution and acid rain caused by power plants. South Korea and Taiwan suffer from air and water pollution. The region has significant challenges to address in the development of sustainable societies.

The complexity of East Asia can be overwhelming. In this book, an attempt is made to identify and explain the conditions and issues that are essential for a person to understand this region. Be prepared for unexpected turns and incredible views, like those along the Li River, as you travel through this ancient region and meet its people.

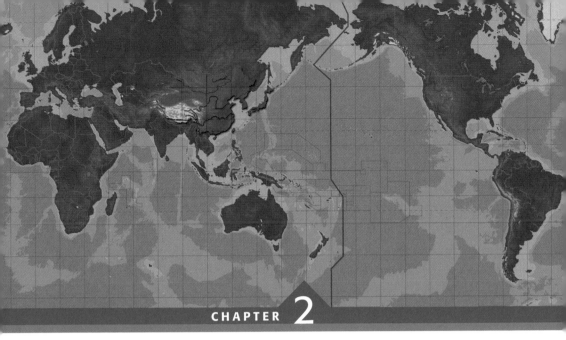

CHAPTER 2

Natural Environment

The natural environment is the foundation on which human activities are built. It provides the essentials of life and presents life-threatening challenges, it can be kind or cruel, and its offerings for human existence can be abundant or meager. East Asia's diverse environmental conditions present a kaleidoscopic array of opportunities and hurdles. In this chapter, you will learn how culture and nature have affected one another in this region of the world.

A WORLD APART

Cultures develop over very long periods of time. In some locations, as in the Middle East and the European culture realm, culture has evolved in a location that is a focal point for cultural diffusion—

the flow of people, ideas and materials from place to place. Others, such as Africa south of the Sahara and South Asia, have developed in relative isolation. This has been the case with East Asia, a region surrounded by some of Earth's most formidable barriers.

As described elsewhere in this book, the "heart and soul" of East Asia have been the fertile river valleys and plains of eastern China. This is where "Oriental" culture took root and thrived. To the east lies the vast expanse of the world's largest (early) barrier, the Pacific Ocean. To the west stretch thousands of miles of parched desert and towering mountains. The north is bordered by the sprawling and desolate Siberia, and to the south is the all-but-insurmountable barrier formed by the Plateau of Tibet and the Himalayas and other mountain ranges. The isolation provided by these barriers made it possible for East Asia to evolve as a unique cultural realm.

It would be a mistake, however, to think of East Asia as a monolithic culture in which all people share a common way of life. Sharp regional differences exist, and many of these, too, can be explained at least in part by environmental conditions. Rather than "determining" culture, the environment offers challenges and opportunities to which people respond in different ways. To the east, on the islands of Japan, water created a barrier that allowed the Japanese to develop a distinct culture. The same holds true on the Korean Peninsula, where people remained relatively isolated from outside influences through time. In Mongolia and western China, people became well adapted to parched desert environments.

THE LAND

The land area of East Asia is a little more than 4.5 million square miles (11.7 million square kilometers), slightly larger than Canada. Like Canada, however, much of the area—perhaps as much as 75 percent of the land—supports very little economic activity and population densities are very low. In both Canada and East Asia, hundreds of thousands of square miles are all but inaccessible, not reached by highway or rail. Lands are too high, too dry, too cold, too remote, or too difficult in some other way to develop economically. There is one huge difference between the two regions, however: Canada's population is about 32 million, whereas East Asia is home to more than 1.5 billion people, 1.3 billion in China alone. This means that nearly one-quarter of the world's population lives in and feeds itself from an area smaller than the United States east of the Mississippi River!

In terms of land and productivity, East Asia can best be thought of as a huge doughnut. The hole represents the highly fertile, moist river valleys and plains that stretch from southern to northern China along the eastern margins of the country. The doughnut itself (with a few small bites taken out, representing plains on the edge) is the "too" lands described in the previous paragraph. With few exceptions, they are areas with natural environments that are difficult to develop economically. Those exceptions include small yet highly fertile valleys and limited areas of coastal plain in Taiwan and Japan and on the Korean Peninsula. In these small areas exist some of Earth's highest population densities. Consider, for example, Japan's population of 128 million people. Japan occupies an area of about 146,000 square miles (378,000 square kilometers), roughly the same as California. Only about 17 percent of Japan is relatively flat and heavily populated—an area about the size of West Virginia. Can you imagine nearly half of all Americans living in that small state? Similar conditions occur in the other countries of East Asia.

As you can imagine, with these diverse land features, East Asia offers some incredibly spectacular—as well as unique—terrain. Japan and Taiwan lie on the Pacific Ocean's Ring of Fire—a zone of geologic instability in which volcanic and seismic (earthquake) activity is common. Natural hazards are addressed later in this chapter. In this context, the zone is important because nearly all of Japan is formed by volcanic mountain tops that reach above sea level. Some, such as the majestic Mount Fuji, rank among the world's most beautiful natural landscapes.

Southern and western China include some of Earth's most difficult landscapes. Here, the "Roof of the World," the Plateau of Tibet, reaches well above 10,000 feet (3,050 meters) to form a cold, windswept, near-wasteland. In the Himalayas, China has all or part of several peaks that rise higher than 25,000 feet (7,620 meters), crowned by the towering Mount Everest (shared with Nepal) which, at 29,035 feet (8,859 meters), is the world's highest mountain.

To the north, a series of rugged mountains and plateaus form an almost solid barrier. They are not as high in elevation as those to the south, but these rugged landscapes, like those of the south, do not favor productive economic land use or human settlement. As a result, very few transportation linkages join East Asia to neighboring lands.

Much of central China and portions of southern Mongolia have relatively flat terrain. Here, millions of years of erosion in the highlands has transported and deposited thousands of feet of sand and silt on basin floors. In the arid climate, much of this material forms the sand dunes of the Taklimakan (or Takla Makan) and Gobi deserts. On the vast expanse of these plains, camels of the ancient Silk Road earned their title "ships of the desert" as caravans carried silk toward markets located thousands of miles to the west.

Two landscapes deserve special mention. In the far southern reaches of China, inland from Hong Kong, karst topography—solution weathering of limestone rock—has created some of the world's most unique and spectacular scenery (described in Chapter 1). Here, the land has been carved into hundreds of steep-sided dome-shaped features that rise as lonely sentinels above surrounding river plains. This region is one of China's major tourist destinations.

To the north, in the vicinity of the great bend of the Huang (Yellow) River, is the world's largest area of loess deposits. This

A camel caravan navigates the desert in China. Camels of the ancient Silk Road earned their title "ships of the desert" as caravans carried silk toward markets located thousands of miles to the west.

very fine, powderlike material was deposited thousands of years ago by winds that picked up and transported fine material lain down by glacial outwash. The river and the Yellow Sea, into which it flows, take their name from the silt picked up by erosion as the river passes through the region.

CLIMATE AND ECOSYSTEMS

All of East Asia lies in the temperate middle latitudes. With the exception of Japan's northern island of Hokkaido, almost the entire region falls within one of three climatic zones and their related ecosystems. In a broad belt that extends from southeastern to northeastern China and includes Taiwan, Japan,

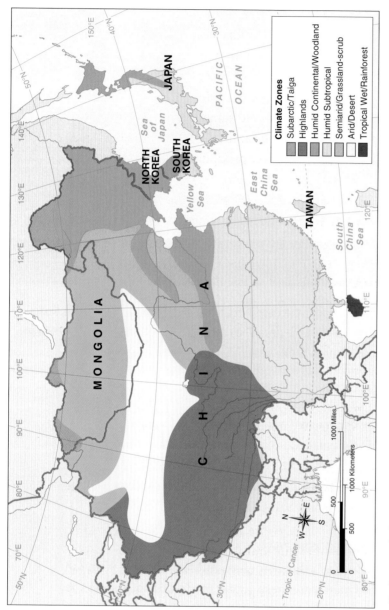

Climate Zones

Subarctic/Taiga
Highlands
Humid Continental/Woodland
Humid Subtropical
Semiarid/Grassland-scrub
Arid/Desert
Tropical Wet/Rainforest

All of East Asia lies in the temperate middle latitudes. In a broad belt that extends from southeastern to northeastern China and includes Taiwan, Japan, and Korea, conditions are humid and subtropical. In Mongolia and central and western China, desert landscapes prevail.

and Korea, conditions are humid and subtropical. Moisture is adequate to support lush vegetation and crop production. Temperatures are warm and humid in the summer and cool and slightly drier in the winter. Frost is rare in the south, where the long growing season allows two rice crops per year. Because the region has been inhabited for thousands of years and the population density is high, very little original vegetation remains. Most natural animal life also has been eliminated. Clearly, human activity dominates nature.

Moving inland to Mongolia and central and western China, desert landscapes prevail. Here, precipitation is scant, with an area about the size of the 48 contiguous U.S. states receiving less than 10 inches (25 centimeters) of moisture per year and much less in some places. In summer, temperatures often soar to well above 100°F (38°C). Under such conditions, few plants or animals can survive. Scattered here and there are pockets of hardy plants that are well adapted to conditions of aridity. On the desert margins and the lower slopes of mountains, grasslands support a largely nomadic grazing lifestyle. In a few places, where good water is available at the surface, oases form lush islands of greenery and life in the otherwise lifeless landscape.

Finally, in much of East Asia, elevation is the primary determinant of weather and climate. Temperatures on average decline about 3.5°F (slightly more than 1°C) with each 1,000-foot (300-meter) change in elevation. To illustrate the importance of elevation for temperature, the Plateau of Tibet, although located at the same latitude as the American "Sunbelt," has temperatures comparable to those of Greenland!

Climate and vegetation are important influences on soil type and potential agricultural productivity. In this regard, China, the Koreas, and Japan are extremely fortunate. Good soils, flat land, and adequate moisture have blessed small portions of each country. These conditions have helped make some of the world's most productive agriculture possible.

ENVIRONMENTAL HAZARDS

Few places in the world can match East Asia in terms of the variety and magnitude of nature's occasional wrath. East Asia ranks at or near the top in the frequency of and destruction resulting from six of nature's most violent events: earthquakes, volcanic eruptions, tsunamis (incorrectly called tidal waves), typhoons (hurricane-like storms), earth flow or slide, and flooding. A huge earthquake that occurs in an uninhabited area causes little damage in human terms. In East Asia, such events occur frequently in some of the world's most densely populated areas. As a result, they can cause horrendous property damage and loss of life. Japan is the country most constantly threatened by each of the hazards cited above. Because of its vulnerability, the country is the world leader in natural hazard research, forecasting, and protection.

Geologic Hazards

A huge zone of geologic instability surrounds almost all of the Pacific Basin. Within this Ring of Fire, as it is called, approximately 80 percent of the world's earthquakes and volcanic eruptions occur. Japan and Taiwan sit squarely on this zone. Japan, in particular, frequently experiences both hazards. In addition, violent events that happen on the ocean floor can cause devastating tsunamis.

Most of East Asia's volcanic activity is limited to Japan. The country has about 40 active volcanoes, 10 percent of the world's total. The country's most volcano-shaped peak, majestic Mount Fuji, appears to be inactive.

Few places on Earth are more prone to seismic (earthquake) activity and destruction than is East Asia. Japan alone averages about more than 1,000 earthquakes each year. In Taiwan, more than 2,200 people were killed by an earthquake in 1999, and in Japan 5,500 people lost their lives in a gigantic earthquake that struck in a very densely populated area in 1995. A 1976 earthquake near Tangshan, China, killed at least 250,000 people (some estimates are much higher). Historically, many more people have lost their lives as a result of earthquakes in East Asia than in the rest of the world combined. The greatest earthquake disaster in history (measured by loss of life) occurred in China's Shaanxi Province in 1556 and resulted in an estimated 830,000 deaths.

Japan's most disastrous earthquake, as measured by loss of life, occurred in 1923. The violent tremor struck the country's most heavily populated area—the cities of Tokyo and Yokohama on the Kanto Plain. The quake's intensity was measured at 8.3 on the Richter scale, comparable to the 1906 earthquake that devastated San Francisco, California. Tokyo lay in ruins, and as many as 140,000 people lost their lives. The 1995 earthquake that struck the region of Kobe and Osaka caused an estimated 100 billion dollars in property damage. This ranks as the most costly natural disaster in history.

Tsunamis (the word is Japanese and means "harbor wave") are huge waves caused by earthquakes or earth slides on the ocean floor. All lands that lie on the Pacific Ocean are susceptible to tsunami devastation. In East Asia, many huge cities and smaller villages are located on harbors or low-lying coastal plains. As a tsunami approaches the shore and shallow water, the water rises and begins to crest in a series of huge waves that can reach 100 feet (30 meters) in height. Powerful waves can destroy everything in their path as they surge ashore. In 1792, 15,000 people were killed by a tsunami that struck the coast of the Japanese island of Kyushu.

Atmospheric Hazards

All East Asian countries except Mongolia can be affected by the raging winds and drenching rain that accompany typhoons (called "hurricanes" in the Atlantic Ocean). In September 2003, South Korea was hit by a typhoon that killed 84 people and knocked out five nuclear power plants. An average 30 such storms pass through the region each year, often leav-

Few places on Earth are more prone to seismic (earthquake) activity and destruction than is East Asia. The 1995 earthquake that struck the region of Kobe and Osaka caused an estimated 100 billion dollars in property damage. This ranks as the most costly natural disaster in history.

ing death and destruction in their wake. Typhoon winds exceed 75 miles (120 kilometers) per hour and on occasion reach 150 miles (250 kilometers) per hour or even higher. Much Asian housing, built of wood and other very light material to withstand earthquake shocks, is no match for winds of this ferocity. Along coasts, storm surges—huge walls of windblown water—cause more damage than do the winds alone. Inland, severe flooding often is caused by the torrential rains associated with the storms. In hilly and mountainous regions, water-saturated earth frequently gives way and flows downslope as a river of mud, earth creep, or landslides that can destroy everything standing in its way.

Flooding

All areas of East Asia, even the desert regions, are subject to flooding. Flood problems related to typhoons and tsunamis have already been discussed. Through time, flood events have taken millions of lives, left tens of millions homeless, and inflicted billions of dollars in property damage.

River flood damage also has taken a terrible toll, particularly in China. Several factors combine to make parts of the country vulnerable. First is the dense population that clusters on fertile land—much of which is river floodplain. Second, extensive deforestation increases the rate and amount of runoff into streams. Finally, stream dynamics themselves contribute to the problem. The Yangtze River, for example, is the world's third-longest river. Many of its tributaries flow from areas of high precipitation and descend rapidly from highlands. Devastating floods have been a regular occurrence along this river.

In the north, the Huang River flows across a very flat plains region where the river is confined by protective levees. During periods of extremely high water, breaks in the levee can occur. Gushing through the openings, floodwater spreads across thousands of square miles of some of China's most densely populated agricultural land. In 1887, flooding along the Huang caused as many as 2 million deaths. What may be the greatest natural disaster of all time occurred in 1931. A tremendous flood on the Huang took perhaps 4 million lives directly and many more as a result of the famine that followed. No wonder the Huang has been given the nickname "China's River of Sorrow."

THREE GORGES DAM

Human history has been marked by a constant struggle that pits mankind against natural forces. Today, one of history's great environmental battles is taking place on the Yangtze River in China's Hubei Province. Here, the world's largest hydroelectric dam is under construction at a cost estimated as high as 75 billion U.S. dollars. When completed in 2009, the 575-foot- (181-meter-) high dam will create a reservoir that reaches 350 miles (560 kilometers) upstream.

Proponents of the dam cite its positive contributions: flood control on the often unruly river; production of massive amounts of hydroelectric energy, which will help replace air-polluting coal, China's major source of energy; and improved navigation on the Yangtze. The project has many critics, as well. As many as 2 million people will be displaced by the rising waters of the reservoir. Environmentalists cite the loss of wildlife habitat and endangered species; some even believe that the reservoir will cause climatic change in the area. Archaeological sites have been lost, and some of the world's most spectacular scenery will be partially lost. Of greatest concern to some is the fact that the dam is built on an active geologic fault. They fear that a massive earthquake could send a rush of water downstream into one of the world's most densely populated plains.

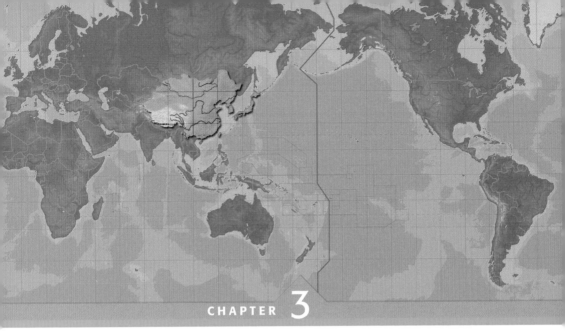

CHAPTER 3

East Asia's Past

China has provided the core of East Asia's history. This ancient society, with roots that trace back thousands of years, is connected historically with each of the other countries in the region. Sometimes these connections were conflicts, and at other times they were cooperative. This history still taints relationships in the region today. Old grudges linger in the region's current dialogs and disagreements. Neighbors are suspicious of China, with its huge size and population, and burning memories of Japan's occupation of China, Taiwan, and the Korean Peninsula linger. Some tensions steeped in historical animosity continue to seethe. They include the bitter disputes between North Korea and South Korea and between

Teeth and skull fragments, dated to at least 500,000 years ago, were discovered in the small village of Zhoukoudian, 30 miles southwest of Beijing. This ancient humanoid was called *Sinanthropus pekinensis*, or Peking Man.

China and Taiwan. Both conflicts keep the region on the brink of renewed military engagement.

Surprisingly, the region has been relatively conflict free for more than two decades, since 1979, when China was at war with neighboring Vietnam. New contacts and communication have helped diffuse some of the old issues. Economic interdependence also is causing these countries to depend more on each other for daily existence. Understanding this complex past requires a story that starts with the very first East Asians.

EARLY HUMANS IN EAST ASIA

The earliest humans discovered thus far in East Asia were located in a small village, Zhoukoudian, located about 30 miles

(48 kilometers) southwest of Beijing. Teeth and skull fragments were found and dated to at least half a million years ago. This ancient humanoid was called *Sinanthropus pekinensis*, or Peking Man. These early people were similar in physique to modern people although they were shorter and their brains were about 80 percent the size of today's human brain. These people used fire and tools that were made of stone and bone. Today, Zhoukoudian is a UNESCO World Heritage site and archaeologists continue to excavate in search of additional clues of early people.

Fossils of a woman and two children that date back 300,000 years have been found on the Korean Peninsula. They were found in lava rock, having been trapped by a volcanic eruption. Tools from even farther back in time, dating to nearly 500,000 years ago, also have been found on the peninsula. These early people struggled to survive in a hostile environment with large animals that preyed on humans.

CHINA
Early History

From these early humans, civilizations developed as long ago as 4,000 years near the Huang River in north China. China today traces its history back to this era, when the roots of language, culture, and political structures began to grow. China is blessed with a long-standing tradition of written history. First composed by people in the ruling and scholar classes, these records provide detail of China's past and the life that existed here during earlier civilizations.

For much of its history, China has been like a sponge: It has soaked up ideas, technology, and other culture traits from neighboring peoples. This trait helped China move forward rapidly as new ideas were incorporated and often improved. In turn, many of China's cultural traits, including language and some technology, were spread to neighbors like Vietnam, Korea, and Japan.

Xia Dynasty

In about 2,000 B.C., the Xia Dynasty developed in China. For centuries, many historians believed that this culture was a myth—that legends had been repeated so many times that they had become "fact." Legends and some writings suggest that there were 17 kings over 14 generations. Other than some written records and oral legends, there was little hard evidence to support the existence of Xia. This changed in 1959, however, when excavations at Erlitous, in the city of Yanshi, China, turned up archeological evidence of the Xia Dynasty. Since that time, cities, bronze tools, art, and tombs have been unearthed to provide confirmation of Xia's existence.

Shang Dynasty

Xia was followed by the Shang Dynasty, which existed from 1700 until 1027 B.C. People of the Shang Dynasty used bronze, jade, and horse-drawn chariots. They protected their cities by putting walls around them to keep intruders out. Inside the walls lived religious and military leaders and nobles. Outside the walls were the peasants, who lived in a much more difficult situation. Agriculture was commonplace, with crops like millet, wheat, and barley harvested. Animals were both hunted and domesticated. Worship of ancestors was practiced, and royalty often was buried with riches. On occasion, common people would be buried alive with royalty, who they were to take care of in the afterlife.

Chopsticks were invented during the Shang Dynasty; a more important development was a writing system. Much of the writing was found on animal bones and turtle shells. Writings on bamboo have not held up well, and many of these artifacts have been lost. The first Chinese calendar was also developed during this era.

The Shang often conducted raids on neighboring villages and cities for the purpose of taking food, livestock, and precious goods. Their bronze weapons and horse-drawn chariots gave them a huge advantage in fighting. As a result, the dynasty wielded military power and was quite successful in conducting raids. After the Shang capital was moved to Yin in 1350 B.C., the dynasty reached its peak of power. The last Shang king, Shang Zhou, committed suicide after his army was defeated by Zhou rebels. This defeat ended the long reign of the Shang Dynasty and served as the beginning of the Zhou Dynasty,which had its capital near Xian, China, in the city of Hao.

Zhou Dynasty

The Zhou Dynasty survived longer than any other Chinese rule; is lasted from 1027 until 221 B.C. The Zhou Dynasty is recognized as the first civilization to unite most of the area now known as China. This period is very important in Chinese history because much of the contemporary culture was shaped then. Confucianism and Taoism started during this era, and great advances were made in military and political thinking. Literature written during this period is still read today. Technology also leaped forward with advancements in astronomy, physics, astrology, mathematics, and medicine. The medical procedure known as acupuncture was developed during the Zhou period, as were technologies such as advanced irrigation systems, use of fertilizers, the compass, and many others.

Han Dynasty

After a period of war in China, the Han Dynasty came to power; it lasted from 206 B.C. to A.D. 220. Work on the world's greatest man-made barrier, the Great Wall of China, begun during the Zhou period, continued into the Han Dynasty and later civilizations. The Great Wall was not constructed as one solitary barrier; rather, it is a series of connecting walls with the last parts built during the Ming Dynasty (A.D. 1368–1644). The protective barrier stretches 4,163 miles (6,700 kilometers) from east to west. One of the great wonders of the world, it was built as a fortification against enemies primarily from present-day

Begun during the Zhou dynasty (1027–221 B.C.), the Great Wall of China was not constructed as one solitary barrier; rather, it is a series of walls with the last parts built during the Ming Dynasty (A.D. 1368–1644). The protective barrier stretches 4,163 miles (6,700 kilometers) from east to west.

Mongolia. Some parts of the wall are now falling into disrepair, whereas others, such as the wall at Badaling, near Beijing, have been repaired and serve as key tourist destinations.

The Han Dynasty started when Liu Bang defeated the Qin army in 206 B.C. The dynasty's leaders incorporated more of the thinking of Confucius into their political structure and daily life. The Han worked to consolidate smaller kingdoms into China in an effort toward unification. These efforts pushed into Vietnam and Korea as the dynasty grew larger under Wu Ti. Wu Ti was a strong military leader and strategist who moved Chinese people into the regions that were seized.

Significant developments during the Han Dynasty included creation of the Silk Road. First created for military purposes, the road became a major highway for trading silk to Middle Eastern and even Roman buyers. Silk was valuable, and China is where silk was developed and the silk industry started to flourish. The road also served as a virtual information highway: People who traveled along the route exchanged information and ideas. When sea routes to Asia were discovered by Europeans in the fifteenth century, the Silk Road became less important because it was easier and more profitable to move goods by ship than overland.

The Han also discovered the usefulness of crop rotation and developed iron tools and weapons. Other inventions included the wheelbarrow, seismograph (for determining the strength of earthquakes), and paper. China was rapidly becoming a very advanced civilization by time of the Han Dynasty.

China Extends Its Reach

Influence of the Han Dynasty reached to Korea, where the Koguryo (Goguryeo) Kingdom was the first to come in contact with the Chinese. This Kingdom was located near today's Chinese and North Korean border. The Koguryo Kingdom existed from 37 B.C. to A.D. 668. It borrowed liberally from the Chinese in architecture and adopted Buddhism as a philosophy of life. Today, China and Korea claim this culture as common thread of their history.

The Koguryo Kingdom—along with the Baekje and Silla kingdoms—represent what is called the "Three Kingdoms era" in Korean history. Baekje was founded by King Onjo in 18 B.C. and Silla by Bak Hyeokgeose in 57 B.C. The kingdom of Baekje was located in southwest Korea, and Silla was located in the southeastern area of the peninsula. The long era of the Three Kingdoms in Korea ended when Silla conquered Baekje in A.D. 660 and Koguryo in A.D. 668. The time period after 668 is often called the Unified Silla Kingdom; it lasted until 935, when it fell to Koryo.

China's fingers continued to reach in other directions under the Jin, Sui, and Tang dynasties. The Jin Dynasty ruled from A.D. 265 to 420, the Sui from 581 to 617, and the Tang from 618 to 907. As in the Zhou and Han dynasties, there were eastern and western Jin dynasties that held almost the entire modern area of China together. Contact between Japan and China had started during the Han Dynasty. During succeeding generations, exchanges between them brought considerable influence to Japan from China's complex culture. Chinese culture accepted by the Japanese included the written language, political institutions and procedures, Buddhism, Confucianism, and even the calendar. Many Japanese were sent to China to study and learn more about Chinese ideas and philosophy. These people returned to Japan and worked to bring reform and advancements.

The Tang Dynasty started in 618. This era was marked by a China that had emerged as an important player on the international scene. China was becoming an international trade center, and merchants came from many distant lands to barter and learn from the Chinese. Even though Buddhism started in India, it began to flourish in China during the Tang Dynasty. A civil service system based on Confucian philosophy was installed to bring the best and the brightest into government. This policy ensured long-term government stability during times of turmoil. It also served as a link between common people and the ruling class. Elements of this civil service structure remained in China's government until 1911.

The Tang Dynasty started dissolving in the mid–eighth century. By the early tenth century, China had been carved up into more than a dozen smaller kingdoms. In 960, the Song Dynasty reunified the country; it controlled most of the lands of modern China until 1127. Then, invaders from the north pushed the Song rulers into the south, where they ruled until 1279. The civil service continued and extended its importance during the Song Dynasty as cities began to develop. The cities

Most Buddhist monks came to China from India and Central Asia by way of the Silk Road. As the westernmost Chinese station on the route, Dunhuang became the ideal place for these foreign monks to learn the Chinese language and culture before entering central China. There are several sites of Buddhist caves in the Dunhuang region, with anywhere from 2 to 492 caves at each site.

became centers of industry and hubs for agricultural activity, government, and trade. Confucianism was even more important during this time than during the Tang Dynasty as scholars applied the teachings to political and philosophical questions of the day. The renewed interest in Confucianism also spread to Korea and Japan, where intellectuals drew on the teachings in efforts to better understand daily life.

The Song Dynasty had what at the time were the world's best ships and navigational skills. The magnetic compass aided navigation, and adoption of a rear rudder vastly improved maneuverability. Gunpowder also was developed during the Song Dynasty. With the great advantages afforded by gunpowder and unsurpassed naval strength, China could be a strong military power. Surprisingly, however, this did not happen. The Song abided by their Confucian religious philosophy that held military power in low esteem. This thinking contributed to the defeat of the Song Dynasty when it was confronted by more militaristic regimes in the region.

The Mongol Era

In 1210, Mongol warriors attacked the Song, and, by 1279, they had expanded their empire into China. This era was called the Yuan Dynasty; it was the first rule of China by foreigners.

By the mid–thirteenth century, the fierce Mongols had become a gathering force in Eurasia (the Europe and Asia landmass). Under the leadership of the legendary Genghis Khan, they had moved into China and Central Europe. The Mongols' reach was staggering for that time period. They swept into all of China under Kublai Khan, the grandson of Genghis Khan, and extinguished the Song Dynasty.

Mongol rule over China lasted until 1368. The period was marked by difficulties in governance because of the language and other cultural differences that existed. While the Mongols held political control, life for much of Chinese society was often better. Punishments were less severe than they had been under the Song Dynasty, and intellectuals and artists were free to express themselves. Theater, opera, and the novel developed during this era as Chinese arts flourished. Marco Polo visited Mongol China during his travels from Venice, and he described the wonders that he saw. Sadly, China's riches were rapidly depleted by the Mongols. During their era of control, they spent lavishly and conducted an expensive, though unsuccessful, military campaign against Japan. By 1368, domestic insurrections had overthrown the Mongols. China was once again back in the hands of the Chinese.

The Ming and Qing Dynasties

Hongwu was a peasant who led the revolt against the Mongols in the fourteenth century. After achieving victory, he rose from being a simple peasant to emperor of China. His rule marked the beginning of the Ming Dynasty, which lasted until 1644. The capital under Hongwu was Nanjing, but it was soon moved to Beijing, where it remains today. Hongwu decreased taxes for peasants and helped improve their lives by increasing food supplies that were stored for use in hard times.

The novel as an art form advanced during this time. Stories written during this era provide foundations for Chinese literature that is treasured today. Encyclopedias and dictionaries developed during this time reveal all types of information about China of this era. The Ming Dynasty used the Great Wall to keep out invaders from the north, although the Mongols continued to be a threat. At the same time, Japan was gaining strength. It had attacked Chinese coastal cities and conducted incursions into Korea. Internal squabbling led to the downfall of the Ming Dynasty. China's second era of foreign rule was about to be presided over by the Manchus, who established the Qing Dynasty.

The Qing Dynasty lasted from 1644 to 1911 and represents the last foreign dynasty to rule in China. Manchuria is now the part of China that lies northeast of Beijing between the Korean Peninsula and Russia. Manchurian rule lasted nearly three centuries. The Manchus kept in place much of the government of the Ming Dynasty but modified it by having both a Manchu and Chinese person hold the same office. The Manchu had more power. This worked reasonably well because the Manchus were not harsh rulers and lowered taxes even further. The dual appointments to government positions also helped reduce internal resistance to the rule of the Manchus.

As China prospered in the peaceful first decades under the Manchus, the arts continued to flourish, with poetry becoming more popular. Later, under ruler Qianglong, the Manchus expanded their country's borders to include Taiwan and even remote Tibet. The Manchus feared both conquerors from outside and conspirators from within the country; thus, they worked diligently to secure their rule from takeover by others.

International trade became important again during the early years of this era because commerce was strong and prosperity reached its highest level during the rule of Qianglong. A major reason that the Manchus found success in ruling in China was that they kept many Chinese ways. Extreme change would have been rejected and made ruling difficult. Instead, the Manchus adopted much of Chinese culture even before they conquered the country. Undoubtedly, this made the Manchus more successful in ruling as outsiders than the Mongols were.

Internal uprisings against the Manchu government were squelched in the late 1700s and early 1800s. European powers were starting to affect China more directly in the nineteenth century, however, with the continuing presence of the British. The Manchus had successfully prevented land attacks and internal rebellions, but they were not prepared for an approach by sea. China's silk and tea were coveted by the British, but the country had little to trade that the Chinese desired.

This changed when the British started to send opium to China. Introduction of this drug caused huge problems. Many Chinese became addicted, and some farmers began to grow more lucrative opium poppies instead of food crops. The Qing Dynasty ended opium trade in 1839. This move triggered the first Opium War with England, which ended in 1842 with the British winning easily. The Treaty of Nanjing ended the war. In defeat, China was forced to cede Hong Kong to the British and open up five ports to trade with the victors. China lost a second Opium War to the British in the 1850s. This defeat forced it to open 11 more ports. In addition to England, the United States, France, and Russia were parties to the unequal treaty that ended the second war and resulted in the British virtually controlling China.

The Qing Dynasty was in a difficult state after the Treaty of Nauking (1842), the supplementary Treaty of Bogue (1843), and the Treaty of Tianjin (1858), which followed the Opium Wars. It began to make an effort to learn more about Western technology. This effort to modernize is referred to as the Self-Strengthening Movement. Unfortunately, it was largely unsuccessful. China had not evolved politically as had Western nations—Japan was more successful in Westernizing than China was. This made the island country a greater threat to the weakened Qing Dynasty. This threat became reality in the short Sino-Japanese War of 1894–1895, which Japan won. China was forced to give up Taiwan and other islands in the terms of the war-ending treaty. China was also forced to recognize Japan's control of the Korean Peninsula.

By the dawn of the twentieth century, the Qing Dynasty was in freefall decline. Rulers had become younger and younger; the last was only two years old when he became emperor in 1909. Foreigners were picking China apart. Not only did Japan receive the spoils of war, but the British increased the size of their Hong Kong holdings to include adjacent areas called the New Territories. Germany, France. Russia and Belgium secured areas of influence in China, and, in 1899, the United States initiated an Open Door policy that sought equal access to China's ports. In addition, internal rebellions had taken their toll on the ruling regime. All of this created an opportunity for change that started with the fall of the last emperor in 1911.

JAPAN

Legend holds that Japan was created by two gods who descended from heaven to create the islands. From this heavenly beginning, Jammu became the first human emperor of Japan in 660 B.C. He started the present-day imperial lineage that claims an unbroken chain tracing back to the Sun Goddess, which gives rise to Japan's descriptive name, Land of the Rising Sun.

The Kofun (A.D. 300–645) and Asuka (538–710) periods overlapped and were both marked by many elements borrowed from China. Japanese rulers sought affirmation of their royal titles from China, which, in turn, recognized Japan's interests on the Korean Peninsula. Elements borrowed from China during these times include Confucianism, etiquette, the calendar, and the written language.

In 710, the imperial palace was moved to the city of Nara, ushering in what is called the Nara period. The capital was patterned after that of the Chinese Tang Dynasty at Chang'an and was home for the emperor until 794, when the capital was moved to Heian, later called Kyoto. This era was called the Heian period, and it lasted nearly 400 years, until 1185. Commercial activity gained momentum during the Nara period; it was centered on the capital city, which grew to more than 200,000 people. Buddhism took root and grew in importance during the Nara period, and Japanese literature rose to new heights. Land ownership systems were also changed. The Nara period was short-lived, though, and its decline was hastened by political infighting as some landowners became more powerful. As the Tang Dynasty weakened in China, Japan's respect for Chinese culture diminished. This started an era during which Japan started to look more inward than outside for answers.

During the Heian period, a process of decentralizing power occurred. Powerful landowning families came to rule large areas of the country. Their power became greater than the emperor's at times. The language also began to change: Japanese adaptations were made to the Chinese written language. At the same time, the visual arts and literature blossomed. The warrior class continued to acquire power and prestige. This group played a large role in the demise of the Heian era and set the stage for the Kamakura period (1185–1333) and the start of Japan's medieval age.

The Kamakura and Muromachi eras (1333–1573) were marked by disunity at the beginning. For some time, there were both northern and southern courts, and the two wrestled for control. Finally, the south gave up, resulting in Kyoto resuming full power in 1392. Feudalism was also a prevalent element in daily life in Japan during those times.

Buddhism and Shinto became very popular during this time, and renewed contact with China brought goods such as silk, porcelain, and books to Japan. Two Mongol invasions from the mainland were repulsed in the late thirteenth century. These victories brought a new spirit of nationalism to Japan. Shinto became even more popular because this native Japanese religion stressed the divine superiority of Japan over other cultures; thus, the rising nationalism that resulted from the defeat of the Mongols contributed to the rise of Shinto, which, in turn, further strengthened national identity.

Western contact with Japan started in 1542, when the Portuguese arrived and introduced Christianity and firearms to the islands. Japanese warlords wanted the weapons, so they also allowed Jesuit missionaries to come and spread Christianity. History shows, however, that, although the guns were readily accepted into Japanese culture, Christianity never gained a foothold in the country.

A warlord named Oda Nobunaga captured Kyoto, the seat of government, in 1568. This started the downfall of the Muromachi rule, which ended five years later. Nobunaga and other warlord successors unified Japan by 1600.

The beginning of the seventeenth century found Japan entering a new era called the Tokugawa, or Edo, period (1600–1867). Tokugawa Ieyasu had overcome all rivals by 1600 and established his capital in the city of Edo (Tokyo). Ieyasu was appointed shogun (military governor) by the emperor and possessed almost unlimited power and wealth. He cleverly redistributed land to loyal feudal land barons called *daimyo*. He then required the daimyo to spend every other year in Edo. This move achieved three things: It kept the daimyo from building local armies to resist the shogun; it reduced the wealth of the daimyo, because residence in Edo was costly; and, finally, it kept the daimyo close at hand, where the shogun could watch over them. Ieyasu's rule began two centuries of stability in Japan.

Japan Closes Its Doors

During the Tokugawa period, Japan closed nearly all its doors to the outside world and trade. Ieyasu did not trust foreigners, particularly Christians bent on spreading their faith. By 1635, Japanese were prohibited from traveling outside of Japan and foreign books were banned. In 1639, the country closed its doors to all foreign trade except for some limited activity with the Netherlands and China that was permitted in the port of Nagasaki. Christians were persecuted: Thousands were killed in 1629 as the country worked to rid itself of outside influences. Japan's door was now almost completely shut and would not reopen for more than two centuries.

As Japan turned inward during the Tokugawa period, important developments were happening within the country. Urbanization was becoming an important trend: Cities such as Osaka, Kyoto, and Tokyo grew rapidly. By the mid-1700s, Tokyo had a population of more than one million people. Handicraft industries sprouted up in these urban areas, and Tokyo became a center for production of food and consumer goods.

Renewed interest in Confucianism took hold in the Edo period and was especially important to the noble warrior class known as the *samurai*. *Bushido* was their code of living; it included the ideas of loyalty, self-discipline, and honor. The samurai worshipped their country and their emperor. Because of their integrity and faithfulness, they ranked highest in Japan's feudal social system. The samurai played a very important role in Japan's history, as was portrayed in the motion picture *The Last Samurai*.

Confucianism provided standards for everyday living, but Shinto remained important and served as a link to national identity. The intertwined nature of Shinto and nationalism exhibited itself in new and more damaging ways in the twentieth century as the religion and government became more closely tied.

The Tokugawa period ended not from within. Rather, the door finally was opened by the West. Western nations had been encroaching on Japan's shores since the start of the eighteenth century, when Russian, British, and even American naval ships and whalers entered Japan's waters. In 1853, Japan changed forever when four U.S. ships commanded by Matthew C. Perry entered Tokyo Harbor and forced the Tokugawa government to open more ports to outsiders. This started the restoration of power to the emperor, a young man named Mutsuhito, who ascended to the throne in 1867. Riding into power under a wave of support for imperial leadership, the Meiji Restoration—one of the most important events in Japan's history—began in 1868 under the young emperor.

Japan Becomes a World Power

Mutsuhito's rule during the Meiji Restoration sought to acquire military weapons and technology comparable to that of the West. This upgrading was intended to develop Japan into a world-class international power. The class system, including the samurai, was abolished, and private ownership of land finally was permitted. A number of other reforms based on Western ideas included the development of a stock market and a market economy. Telegraphs, roads, railroads, weapons factories, shipyards, and other economic and infrastructure developments improved the country's military abilities. Foreign military leaders were brought in to teach military strategy. Universal military service was installed, and some personnel were sent abroad to learn more about military strategy and planning. Shinto increasingly emphasized the worship of the emperor and the national identity of the Japanese. Soon after the Meiji Restoration, Japan's economic and military machines were working at top speed.

China and Japan fought the Sino-Japanese War in 1894–1895. Japan won and claimed Taiwan as the spoils of war. Russia was defeated in 1904–1905 in another war that provided Japan with more influence in Korea. This was a significant victory because it marked the first time an Asian country had defeated a European power. Japan annexed Korea in 1910 because its military machine was well oiled and operating efficiently. In response to these victories, Japanese nationalism intensified and became a problem for the ruling government. In 1912, Emperor Mutsuhito died. The resulting change in leadership brought about disastrous results for Japan.

KOREA

Korea was influenced by its neighbors, such as the Chinese cultural impact during the period of the Three Kingdoms. After the Silla Dynasty united the peninsula, the Koryo Dynasty came to power and ruled until 1392, an interrupted period of Mongol rule. The name Korea is drawn from this dynasty. After years of fighting during the early Koryo era, a period of rapid progress that somewhat paralleled the Song Dynasty in China started. The roots of many of Korea's martial arts can be traced back to this time period. Movable type was invented in 1234, more than 200 years before it appeared in Europe. Trade links established with China and with Buddhism and Confucianism stimulated the thinking of the day. Korea, however, seemed to be under constant threat of invasion by its neighbors.

In 1231, at the peak of Koryo civilization, Mongols invaded the peninsula. After gaining control of the region, the Mongols enlisted the aid of locals in their failed attempts to invade Japan. The Mongols finally were expelled from Korea in the fourteenth century by the Chinese and local rebels. The Chosun Dynasty began then; it lasted more than five centuries, from 1392 to 1910, making it one of the longest-reigning dynasties in history.

General Yi Song-gye became the first emperor of the new dynasty in 1392. He immediately embarked on reforming landownership practices. Buddhist temples and monks controlled vast tracts of land during the Koryo period. They lost power with the land reforms that took place under Yi. This meant that the popularity of Buddhism started to decline during the early Chosun period. At the same time, Confucianism started to become more influential—the new leaders embraced this philosophy and rejected Buddhism. There was much resentment of Buddhist monks because they had wielded political, economic, and social power during the Koryo period and many had become corrupt in their practices. The land reforms and persecution of monks were popular with the peasants, who viewed Buddhism as a primary cause of their previous problems. No enduring new religion was introduced to replace Buddhism during the Chosun era. This contributed to the secular (not religious) nature of both Koreas today.

The Chosun era also brought a renaissance in the sciences, arts, and the development of new technology. Seoul became the permanent capital city in 1394, when King Yi Song-gye moved to the city and started construction on the capital. *Hangul* was established as the Korean alphabet by King Sejong in 1443, and it serves as the basis for today's written Korean language. Leaders after Sejong were weaker, and thus Korea became susceptible to outside attacks by the Japanese and Manchus in the sixteenth and seventeenth centuries, respectively. Although repelled, the attacks caused substantial damage to Chosun's agricultural land and economy, a condition that furthered the region's decline.

Throughout the eighteenth century, Western ideas entered Chosun by way of China. Direct contact was discouraged because of the feared impact of Catholic missionaries, who were viewed negatively. Most Western incursions for trading or other purposes were rejected in the early nineteenth century. Chosun basically closed its doors to outsiders. This changed in1876, when Japan forced an unequal treaty on the Koreans. Korea tried to neutralize the effects of this treaty by signing treaties with Italy, Great Britain, Russia, the United States, and others in late nineteenth century. When Japan defeated China in 1895 and Russia in 1905, however, the door was open for Japan to increase its control over the Korean peninsula.

The Chosun era ended abruptly when Japan invaded the peninsula in 1910. Foreigners once again ruled Korea. How long would this occupation last and how would it affect the Koreans? These and other questions will be answered in Chapter 4.

MONGOLIA

Mongolia reached the zenith of its power more than five centuries ago. Starting with Genghis Khan, Mongolia established a pattern of warfare and developed outstanding warriors. European and other armies were slow and wore heavy protective military garb, but the Mongols rode horses and executed quick and well-coordinated attacks. They had superb communication in the field, and warriors were excellent marksmen. They were well disciplined and very effective fighters. All of this prepared the Mongols well for conquering others.

The Mongol invasions of China and Korea and attempted invasion of Japan were mentioned earlier in this chapter. The breadth of the Mongol Empire has not been mentioned, however. At one time, it reached farther than any other empire in history. By 1241, expeditions had reached not only into China and Korea, but also into Russia and as far west as today's countries of Hungary, Lithuania, Italy, Austria, and Poland. At the height of the Mongol incursion into central Europe, leaders were summoned back to Mongolia. The khan had died, and protocol demanded that his offspring return to elect the new khan. Later, all of China was conquered by Kublai Khan, which ushered in the Mongol-controlled Yuan Dynasty.

Why did the Mongol Empire eventually collapse? The answer lies in part in the empire's vast size, which made governance difficult. Another contributing factor was that the Mongols did not culturally or socially absorb the conquered peoples.

Finally, and perhaps most important, there were not enough Mongols to rule the conquered lands. Local populations almost always exceeded those of the ruling Mongols.

After the fall of the Yuan Dynasty, many Mongols returned home. Shortly afterward, civil war broke out among Mongol factions, but the Mongols remained strong enough to threaten China again during the Ming Dynasty. When the Mongols did not have others to fight, they often fought among themselves; tribal animosities often resulted in bloody conflict.

By the seventeenth century, the Mongols were threatened in the east by Manchus, in the south by the Chinese, and in the north by Russians. Mongolia entered an era in which bordering regional powers began to exert strong influence over this remote and barren land. By 1691, the Manchus had established military control over much of Outer (northern) Mongolia, thereby ending the region's independence. Inner (southern) Mongolia was eventually absorbed by China. The Mongols tried to rebel against their Manchu and Chinese masters but were unsuccessful until 1911, when a major change happened in China. Today, Outer Mongolia is the independent country of Mongolia, and Inner Mongolia remains part of China.

TAIWAN

Taiwan (Formosa) also fell to outsiders, and the island of Formosa has been under foreign domination many times during its past. The Portuguese, Spanish, and Dutch all arrived on Formosa's shores in the sixteenth and seventeenth centuries, and the Dutch finally prevailed. They were followed by the Taywan Kingdom, which lasted only from 1662 to 1683, when the Manchus annexed the island onto China. The island remained a part of China until the end of the Sino-Japanese War in 1895, when it was ceded to Japan. It remained under Japanese control until the end of World War II.

The history of East Asia is complex and marked by many conflicts and shifting borders. Mongols, Manchus, Chinese, Japanese, and Koreans have all had civilizations that rose to great heights. At the dawn of the twentieth century, the region was affected by Japan's rise to power and increasing Western influences. Chapter 4 explores the region during the often-turbulent past century.

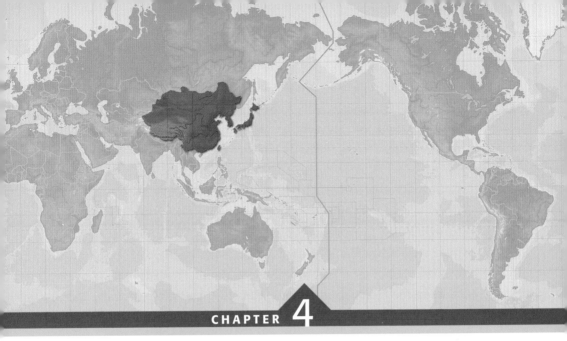

A Century of Transition and Change

At the dawn of the twentieth century, East Asia found itself in a difficult situation. China had been infiltrated by the influence of foreigners and was weakened. Korea had fallen under the control of Japan, the new power in the region. Victories over China in 1895 and Russia in 1905 and the invasion of Korea in 1910 left Japan the strongest player and a new world power. Taiwan also was under the control of Japan, having been ceded to the Land of the Rising Sun by China after it lost the Sino-Japanese War.

Would the twentieth century continue to be an era of outside influence, regional fighting, and neighbors conquering neighbors, as was the pattern in earlier centuries? Would democracy find its way into this region, where it had achieved very limited success in the past? Was this region heading toward new opportunities or drifting toward disaster? All of these are important questions that set the stage for this complex chapter in East Asia's historical geography.

CHINA AND MONGOLIA TAKE NEW DIRECTIONS

The new century found dissatisfaction with existing Chinese rule, which had proven ineffective. Dr. Sun Yat-sen was a reformer who advocated "Three Principles of the People": nationalism, democracy, and people's livelihood. The nationalist idea was aimed at pushing out the Manchus, and the principle of democracy was advocated to bring a popularly elected government to China. The principle of people's livelihood was to promote economic security and land reform. Sun was against the ruling Qing Dynasty and found powerful backers in foreign Chinese who also opposed the existing rulers.

In 1911, a revolution ultimately resulted in Yuan Shikai assuming the provisional presidency of the new Republic of China in January 1912. The last Qing emperor abdicated the throne in February. Yuan Shikai was a military leader and soon demonstrated that he was not a believer in democratic rule. He seized more power and became dictatorial. This resulted in the formation of Kuomintang (KMT), or National People's Party, an opposition party. Elections for the parliament were held in 1913, and the KMT won a majority of seats. Unhappy about the results, Yuan had a KMT leader assassinated. This action propelled resistance against Yuan's rule. He used military force to suppress the rebellion, however, thereby strengthening his grip on the government. Sun Yat-sen was forced to flee to Japan.

As China's president, Yuan had difficulty receiving international recognition. To help persuade the international community to recognize his dictatorial government and to placate Russian interests, Yuan allowed Outer Mongolia to become independent in 1915. Later in 1915, Yuan tried to make himself China's monarch. This resulted in further rebellion, which included resistance from many of his military officers. Yuan died of natural causes in 1916, and few grieved the loss.

Outer Mongolia was still trapped between two strong regional powers, China and Russia, and Inner Mongolia had already been incorporated into China. The remaining area sought protectors. Russia's location made it an obvious potential ally. The Treaty of Kyakhta was signed in 1915 by Russia, China, and Mongolia; it provided for Mongolia's autonomy, although the new country's location was still affected by the huge powers that lay to the north and south. During World War I, Russia was preoccupied by other activities, and its stewardship of Mongolia became less important.

JAPAN FLEXES ITS MILITARY MUSCLE

Japan was the strongest power in East Asia at the start of the twentieth century, and it sought to further expand its influence in the region. The island country found many opportunities to do just that. China was weakened after the death of Yuan. Europe, Russia, and the United States were preoccupied with World War I. In 1915, when conditions were chaotic in China, Japan pushed for the country to become a protectorate. It fought on the side of the Allies in World War I, which allowed it to seize Shandong, a German-held region of China, and other areas in the Pacific. The weakened Chinese government secretly complied with the Japanese claim to Shandong. When the secret was revealed in 1919, massive student demonstrations against both the Chinese and Japanese governments broke out in China. This sparked the return of Sun Yat-sen, who, by 1921, was able to assume control over much of southern China. He also sought support from Russia. Russia complied with this request but played both sides of the fence by supporting not only Dr. Sun but also the Chinese Communist Party (CCP).

Sun died in 1925, and Chiang Kai-shek assumed the leadership of the nationalists and the KMT. Sun had kept the CCP and the KMT together during his later years, but a split started to emerge shortly after his death. Even with the impending split, Chiang Kai-shek unified most of the country by 1928.

Japan had gone though its own turmoil after World War I. The national debt had grown because of the war, and citizens were increasingly dissatisfied with their elected leaders. There were many political parties and weak coalitions in the Diet, Japan's parliament. Because of the fragility of the coalitions, the governments were not able to successfully address the internal problems that were developing during the 1920s. Deflation caused prices to fall, and rice shortages developed, resulting in food riots.

Hirohito became emperor of Japan in 1926. His reign is called the Showa period; *showa* means "enlightened peace." Nationalism was closely linked with Shinto and had been rising for years in Japan. This fervor was fed by the war victories over China and Japan and the land gains that had been made in recent decades. Dissatisfied with ineffective civilian rulers, by the late 1920s, the military began to consolidate its power. Japan invaded and seized Manchuria in 1931 and turned it into a puppet state called Manchukuo. Premier Inukai Tsuyoshi criticized the military's actions, resulting in his assassination. This event marked the end of civilian rule in Japan. The military, fueled by the rising nationalism, now ruled the country.

Japan invaded China in 1937. During the occupation that followed, hundreds of thousands of Chinese were raped, tortured, or killed by ruthless Japanese troops. The rape of Nanking (Nanjing) alone represents one of the greatest atrocities in the history of humankind. Almost 300,000 Chinese were killed in the massacre. More than 20,000 women and children were raped during the siege, and most were then killed.

In addition to the nationalistic influences and military dominance that existed in Japan before World War II, the country required great amounts of natural resources to feed its military and economic machines. With few resources of its own, Japan was forced to find outside sources for oil and other

Japan invaded China in 1937. During the occupation that followed, hundreds of thousands of Chinese were raped, tortured, or killed by ruthless Japanese troops.

strategic items. This meant creating an empire with colonies to supply the necessary resources. In 1939, Japan launched an invasion of Eastern Mongolia, but the attack was repulsed by a combined military force from the Soviet Union and Mongolia. Eighty thousand Japanese were killed in the fighting, but this did not deter Japan's attempt to increase its resource base.

As Europe erupted into World War II in 1939, Japan turned its attention toward Eastern and Southeastern Asia as possible targets for its expansion efforts. A major obstacle to its dream of a Pacific empire was the United States, which had stayed out of World War II but was providing support to the Allies. The United States had a major military presence in the Pacific, with bases in Hawaii and the Philippines. In an attempt to deal the U.S. forces a fatal blow, Japan launched a surprise attack on Pearl Harbor, in Hawaii, on December 7, 1941. Ten hours later, another attack was made on the U.S. base at Manila, in the Philippines. These initial strikes were intended to shell-shock the United States and give Japan a free hand in creating its Asia-Pacific empire.

In short order, the Philippines, Indonesia, Malaya, Burma, Indochina, and Singapore fell to Japan. Japanese forces found stiff resistance in China and Mongolia in the early years of the war, but they controlled large sections of China, all of Manchukuo, and the Korean Peninsula. Japan soon found itself stretched over too vast an area, and with the United States drawn into the war, Japan's early successes turned into disaster. With the sea battle of Midway Island in the Pacific in June 1942, the tide of the war turned in favor of the Allies. Japan and its Axis partners were beginning to lose the conquered lands. In the Asia-Pacific region, the Allies began to island-hop in an effort to push the invaders back toward their homeland.

Japan's occupation of conquered lands had not been a pleasant experience. Koreans, Chinese, and others in Southeast Asia had suffered under their rule before and did so again during World War II. Many women were forced to become "comfort women," or prostitutes, and hundreds of thousands of civilians were forced into labor or killed. The scars from this occupation and the relationships damaged during the war made life difficult for the Japanese after World War II.

The Americans and their allies pushed Japan back to its home islands, and the United States considered an invasion of the country. This was rejected in favor of using a new weapon that scientists had developed: the atomic bomb. On August 6, 1945, the United States became the first country to employ atomic weapons in war by dropping a bomb on the city of Hiroshima. Nearly 100,000 people were killed by the blast or its aftereffects. Despite this show of strength, Japanese aggression continued. Three days later, on August 9, an atomic bomb was dropped on the city of Nagasaki, resulting in 75,000 more deaths. Japan's military leaders still would not surrender, but Emperor Hirohito did. World War II in the Pacific had finally ended, and Japan lay in ruins.

During the last days of World War II, on August 8, 1945, the Soviet Union declared war on Japan. Mongolia declared war on Japan two days later. Soviet and Mongolian forces quickly moved into Inner Mongolia and Manchuria. These late efforts secured the Soviets land concessions from Japan after the war and allowed Mongolia to receive China's recognition of its independence. This was an important component of the Sino-Soviet Treaty of Friendship, Alliance, and Mutual Assistance, which was signed in August 1945.

The war left Japan defeated, devastated, and occupied by the United States under forces led by General Douglas MacArthur. In 1947, the country adopted a new constitution that was drafted by the United States. The document included a provision that renounced war as a tool for resolution of conflicts with other nations. It also developed a parliamentary system, with the Diet serving as the legislative body. The emperor was stripped of most of his powers. He became primarily a symbol of the country, a role similar to that held by the king or queen of England. The American occupation of Japan lasted until 1952.

THE KOREAN PENINSULA

Protests against Japanese rule began shortly after Korea was ceded to Japan in 1910. The Japanese treated the Koreans poorly during their occupation, and this caused resentment to build against the foreign rulers. Because of the resistance, somewhat surprisingly, Japan loosened its grip on Korea during the 1920s. This decade became a time when positive steps were taken in the economic, political, and social arenas. Labor unions organized, and industries started to develop. Even with Japan allowing greater flexibility however, the Koreans considered Japanese rule illegitimate.

Political seeds planted in the early decades of the twentieth century spawned Communism, nationalism, and cries for self-government. These efforts were squelched when the military took control of Japan's government and used Korea as a colony. Korean males were forced into Japan's military, agricultural and mineral resources were used to support Japan's nationalistic interests, and Koreans were required to speak Japanese and attend Shinto services. Japanese discrimination against Koreans included laws that made them second-class citizens. In 1939, Japan forced Koreans to adopt Japanese names. Obviously, all of this increased the Koreans' dislike of Japan and resentment of anything Japanese.

Because of its common border with Korea, Russia had had a long-standing interest that country for security reasons. During the 1920s and later, the Soviet Union developed relationships with Communists in Korea. Korea had often provided a safe haven and training for individuals fighting against the Japanese. One Korean Communist, Kim Il Sung, had been a guerrilla who fought against the Japanese rule. During the war, the Soviet Union and United States agreed to divide Korea at the 38th parallel once hostilities ended. Many Koreans trained by the Soviets moved in to control the area north of the parallel. In response to the perceived Communist threat on the peninsula, the United States countered the Soviet-trained forces by occupying the area south of the 38th parallel. The cold war between the two super-powers had come to the Korean Peninsula.

After World War II, the United States and the Soviet Union began to divide the world into two camps. Korea was firmly caught in the pinching grip of this worldwide conflict. China was becoming a Communist state, and the American fear was that all of Asia might go Communist, as only the small niche in South Korea was outside this sphere. In 1948, with American support, South Korea declared that it was an independent country, the Republic of Korea. Syngman Rhee assumed the presidency. North Korea declared its sovereignty a month later and claimed power over the south. Kim Il Sung was declared premier. By 1950, the Soviet Union was pushing Kim and the North Koreans to go to war to unite the two Koreas. With su-perior military forces, North Korea invaded South Korea on June 25, 1950.

Two months after the start of the war, South Korea's army had been pushed back to a small area on the southeastern coast near Pusan. South Korea asked the United Nations (UN) Secu-rity Council to intervene. At the time, the Soviet Union was boycotting the Security Council to protest Taiwan's seat on this UN body (instead of the People's Republic of China). This boy-cott caused the Soviets to not veto the UN resolution that would send an international force to Korea to stop the invasion. To implement this resolution, U.S. troops and forces from 15 other countries, including Great Britain and Canada, were promptly sent to South Korea. Secretly, they landed forces under General Douglas MacArthur at Inchon, on the peninsula's west coast. The UN forces in Inchon and Pusan moved quickly to cut off North Korean troops from their supply lines.

In two weeks, the UN forces had driven the North Koreans nearly back to the prewar boundaries at the 38th parallel. The

Caught between clashing ideologies of democracy and communism, South Korea (democratic) and North Korea (communist) fought for complete control of the peninsula from 1950 to 1953. After all of the devastation and death caused by the war (nearly 5 million people died), the result was a stalemate with a dividing line at the 38th parallel.

United Nations forces did not stop there. Soon, they had pushed the North Koreans almost back to the Yalu River, the boundary between Korea and China. Uncomfortable with the approaching UN and U.S. forces, China amassed nearly one-third of a million troops to support North Korea. These forces joined the North Koreans and pushed the UN forces back to the south.

In July 1953, the fighting ended with North Korea and South Korea signing a cease-fire agreement. Nearly 5 million people had died in the conflict, and the peninsula was in ruins. Animosity between the Communist North Korea and the democratic South Korea was greater than before the war. After all of the devastation and death caused by the war, the result was a stalemate with a dividing line still at the 38th parallel. The Soviets had turned their interests elsewhere during the war, but China maintained a strong military presence in North Korea until 1958. The United States has kept troops in South Korea ever since the war.

Today, the 38th parallel is designated as a demilitarized zone (DMZ), where no troops from North Korea or South Korea can trespass. The DMZ was established by the armistice agreement that ended the war. It consists of a 151-mile- (243-kilometer-) long corridor that is 2.5 miles (4 kilometers) wide. According to the agreement, incursions by air, land, and sea are forbidden. Since the DMZ was established, however, there have been tens of thousands of violations by North Korea. North Korea has even dug tunnels under the DMZ in an effort to infiltrate South Korea.

The continuing conflict between North Korea and South Korea has relaxed somewhat during recent years. Families divided by the war have been allowed, on occasion, to cross the border to meet other family members. The peninsula remains a global hot spot, however, with North Korea poised to attack South Korea, Japan, and others in the North Pacific with long-range missiles and a growing nuclear threat.

CHANGES IN CHINA

The unity that Chiang Kai-shek brought to China in the late 1920s began to fracture with Japan's seizure of Manchuria and other Japanese intrusions into China. Chinese people became dissatisfied with the rule of Chiang's KMT party, which seemed to be more preoccupied with the Communists than with the Japanese. After a military mutiny that detained him for a number of days in late 1936, Chiang decided to work with the Communists to fight the Japanese. The KMT–Communist united front began to have success against the Japanese, but tension between the two Chinese parties continued.

In the early 1940s, the Communists worked on land reform and winning over rural people. The KMT again pursued the Communists, but Communist leader Mao Zedong encouraged his followers to work and live with the local people. In this way, they would see that the Communists were interested in them and in their way of life. By the end of World War II, the KMT and the Communists were nearly engaged in a civil war. With Russia aiding the Chinese Communists in Manchuria, Communist interests established a firm foothold in that region when the Japanese withdrew. The People's Liberation Army soon gained the upper hand, and, by 1948, the nationalist KMT was in trouble, clinging to power mainly in the cities. This foothold soon was lost, as Beijing fell to the Communists in early 1949 and other cities fell soon afterward. In retreat, Chiang Kai-shek declared that Taiwan would be the temporary capital of China. Mao Zedong established his government on the mainland in the newly named People's Republic of China (PRC).

International recognition of the PRC was slow because many countries, including the United States, had been supporting the KMT. Mao worked to turn China into a socialist economy, but economic growth was painfully slow. Large, communally worked farms called "communes" were not very productive. Soon after Mao died in 1976, steps were taken to make the economy more open and less socialist. By the end of the twentieth century, most socialized aspects of the economy had been dropped and China's economy was booming. The country even had an active stock market.

Political change in China has been much slower since the PRC was founded. Protests have frequently been quashed, as in Tiananmen Square in Beijing in June 1989, when hundreds of people protesting for democracy were killed. Even religious groups such as Falungong have been persecuted in Hong Kong and China because the government perceives these groups as political threats.

Mao proclaims the founding of the PRC. Beijing fell to the Communists in early 1949 and other cities fell soon afterward. Mao Zedong established his government on the mainland in the newly named People's Republic of China (PRC).

THE TWENTY-FIRST CENTURY

By the beginning of the twenty-first century, many countries in East Asia had become strong economic and political powers on the world stage. China's booming economy has become one of the world's strongest, and Japan, the world's third-ranking economic powerhouse, is recovering from the stagnancy displayed during the 1990s. South Korea has steadily made strides to become more democratic. Taiwan has also had a strong economy supported by a strong democratic government. Even isolated Mongolia has shown remarkable progress. Only North Korea seems to be locked in another era: It is a backward military state led by the son of Kim Il Sung, with a failing economy that produces nuclear weapons but cannot feed its own people.

The twentieth century seemed to be divided into two major time periods with differing personalities. The first half, until the end of the Korean War in 1953, was marked by fighting and conflict. The second half was marked by the development of independent countries and rapid economic development in the region. Democracies emerged in Japan, Taiwan, Mongolia, and South Korea, with China and North Korea locked into more dictatorial governments. Which personality will dominate the region during the twenty-first century?

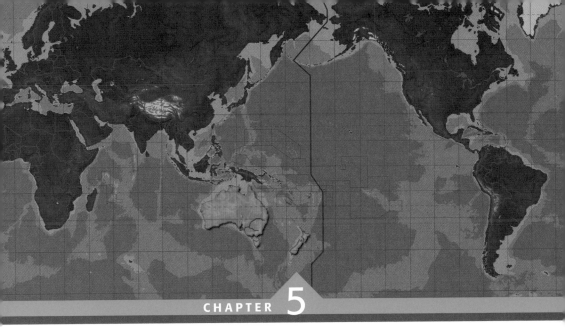

CHAPTER 5

The People of East Asia

In Japan, it is customary for a visitor to remove his or her shoes before entering a person's home. Slippers are provided for the visitor to wear in the house. A separate pair of slippers is provided for use in the bathroom. Thus, the visitor will switch from the house slippers to the bathroom slippers when using the facilities and then switch back when leaving the bathroom. This is only one example of the many cultural traditions that exist in East Asia, a region with thousands of traditions and customs.

From the vast population of China to sparsely populated Mongolia, people are engaged in all of the normal activities of life. Their lives are filled with work and play, family and friends. Some culture traits vary greatly within the region, whereas others are quite similar,

Slippers sit outside a Japanese house. In Japan, it is customary for a visitor to remove his or her shoes before entering a person's home. Slippers are provided for the visitor to wear in the house.

with close historical linkages. In terms of culture trait origins and diffusion (spread), China has had a profound impact on the region. Even Mongolia's influence has swept across many areas in East Asia. All of these historical connections have left cultural remnants in their wake. Most people in this region usually convey a welcoming attitude toward visitors who seek to better understand their culture. This chapter examines the people of East Asia and some of the cultural patterns that exist today. Take off your shoes, put on the slippers, and enter the fascinating world of East Asian culture.

Because of the relative cultural homogeneity within the region, it is important to recognize that each country is culturally unique in many ways. Religions have been adopted and have grown from within these civilizations. Foods, clothing, dance,

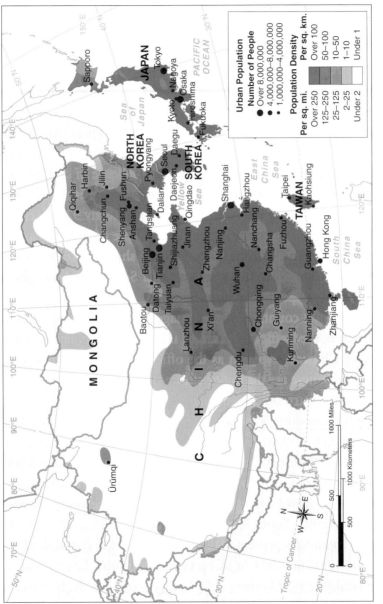

The East Asia region is remarkable for its contrasting populations. China, for example, is the world's most populated country by a wide margin, whereas Mongolia has fewer than 3 million residents. Areas closer to the Pacific Ocean are more densely populated than the arid inland areas, especially western China and Mongolia.

This is a Buddhist temple in Tibet. Buddhism started in India in about 600 B.C. It flourished in China during the Tang Dynasty, which ran from A.D. 618 through the middle of the eighth century, and continues today.

search for material things only causes human suffering. He believed that people should not succumb to worldly desires; if they did, they would need to be reborn into another life. By resisting these desires, they would not need to be reborn into another life of suffering. *Nirvana* is the state that Buddha said did not require rebirth, a state where there was freedom from daily suffering and the cyclical birth and rebirth process. To achieve nirvana, Buddha advocated the Eightfold Path, which teaches believers to believe right, desire right, think right, live right, do the right things, think the right thoughts, behave right, and practice deep reflection.

Buddhism is popular in Mongolia, Taiwan, Japan, and South Korea, so this philosophy affects the daily life of many

East Asians. Even China has a strong Buddhist contingency, which is mostly in Tibet. There, however, government persecution of teachers of Buddhist philosophy remains strong, as was noted in 2004 by the International Campaign for Tibet. Most East Asian Buddhists believe in nonviolence. Buddhists usually worship in their own homes and frequently have statues of Buddha. Five fundamental precepts are held by most Buddhists; they include the following promises:

1. Not to harm or kill any living things
2. Not to steal or take anything that is not freely given
3. To control sexual desires
4. Not to tell lies
5. Not to drink or take drugs

Other Religions

Various Christian denominations, Taoism, and Islam are also practiced in East Asia, but they are not as common as other philosophies and religions. Taoism was founded in China by Lao Tsu, a contemporary of Confucius about 600 B.C. *Tao* translates into "path" or "the way." It started as a philosophy but evolved into a religion. Many other local religious practices exist in East Asia, and people often combine elements from one or more philosophies or religions into their belief structure.

THE ARTS

The arts are part of important traditions in East Asia, where visual arts and music have long played significant cultural roles. With China's history, it should be no surprise that there is a rich cultural heritage in the arts. Religion often inspired artists: Hundreds of Buddhas are carved into solid rock or represented in Chinese sculptures. Elaborate paintings with rich colors show traditional clothing, hairstyles, and daily activities in China and Japan. In Xian, China, there is a silent army of thousands of unique and life-size military figures that were created

China has a number of art forms, including painted pottery, jade figurines, paper cuts, paintings, sculpture, carvings, and calligraphy (the written language itself is used as art). Korea has been strongly influenced by Chinese culture in music, the visual arts, and calligraphy.

out of terra-cotta more than 2,200 years ago. Individual warriors, servants, and horses pulling chariots are today displayed in the collection that may number 8,000.

China has a number of art forms, including painted pottery, jade figurines, paper cuts (an intricate art form first developed in China around the first century A.D.), paintings, sculpture, carvings, and calligraphy (the written language itself is used as art). Japan and other areas in East Asia have also used a wide array of art forms to convey their culture and creativity.

Painting is the preferred visual form of artistic expression in Japan. Paintings may be on ceramics or other surfaces. Often, the work is an expression of other aspects of Japanese culture such as traditional dress, landscapes, or gardens. Sculpture is less evident in Japan's visual arts than in China and usually is linked to religious subjects. Other popular Japanese arts include wood-block prints and origami, which is the creation of animals and other things by folding paper. *Kabuki* (stylized theater) remains a popular performing art in Japan. It features elaborate and colorful costumes that date back to the seventeenth century.

Korea has been strongly influenced by Chinese culture in music, the visual arts, and calligraphy. Sculpture in South Korea reflects ties to Buddhism. Pagodas are found in Korea, as is the visual art of woodcarving. Art in North Korea is very traditional. There, unlike in South Korea, artists are not free to openly express themeslves.

FOODS

East Asia's foods have become popular worldwide. There are few communities of any size that do not offer Japanese, Chinese, or Korean fare, especially in the West. Most of these foods are modified from those overseas and sometimes possess little resemblance to the dish as served in Asia. Thousands of taste delights are offered in this region, and each country has special dishes.

China is well known for its fine cuisine. What is not commonly known in the West is that there are many regional differences in foods. Szechuan (Sichuan) foods are recognized for the use of hot peppers, whereas Shandong cooking is known for seafood. The serving of Chinese food is an art in itself. Entrées are prepared to appeal to the senses—with different textures, colors, smells, and tastes. Some examples of Chinese cuisine are Beijing duck, sweet and sour pork (or fish or chicken), bamboo shoots with snake slices, beggar's chicken (chicken slow cooked with anise and other spices in a clay wrapping that hardens when baked), bean curd, turtle soup, and, of course, rice and noodles. The Chinese often use exotic species such as snakes or civet cats for food. Because it was settled by Chinese after the Communist takeover, Taiwan offers foods from all across mainland China.

Japanese foods have aesthetic appeal similar to that in China. Rice is a staple of the diet, but meat or seafood is often added to fill out the meal. Japanese favorites include *tempura, sushi, sashimi, udon, soba, gyoza, and yakitori*. A popular flavoring is the green-colored paste called *wasabi*, which gives a strong horseradish flavoring to seafood like sushi and sashimi. Ramen is another food enjoyed by Japanese (and Westerners), but its roots are in China. Like the Chinese, the people of Japan use chopsticks when eating.

Many Korean foods are spicy. Red pepper, ginger, green onion, and garlic are commonly used. Most famous among Korean foods is probably the pickled spicy cabbage dish called *kimchi*. Other popular Korean foods include *bulgogi*, or *pulgoki* (Korean barbeque), *maeuntang* (spicy seafood soup), and various dishes made with only vegetables. Chopsticks are used in Korea, and rice serves as a staple of the Korean diet.

Mongolian foods are often high in fat and protein, both of which help Mongolians survive the long, harsh winters. Meats such as camel, beef, lamb, and horse are eaten, and herders sometimes eat boiled animal fat to increase their caloric intake. Although meats are the core of the Mongolian diet, vegetables and other foods such as millet, wheat, and oats are commonly eaten.

Outsiders have been visiting East Asia for centuries, starting with Marco Polo's travel to China; however, the colonial influence of Western countries has been limited to a large extent by East Asia's long periods of "closed doors." Distant international trade may have begun with the Silk Road. Today, East Asia is a

Japanese foods have aesthetic appeal similar to that in China. Rice is a staple of the diet, but meat or seafood is often added to fill out the meal. Japanese favorites include *tempura, sushi, sashimi, udon, soba, gyoza, and yakitori.*

major economic power linked to all corners of the world by a dense network of sea and air routes. Only the hermitlike North Korea has failed to share in the region's rising prosperity and growing linkages with the rest of the world.

Western products, including familiar fast-food outlets and quick-stop convenience stores, are found throughout most of East Asia. Western music is also very popular and readily available in most of the region. The Internet is a universal source of not only information, but also of music files. At the same time, Chinese, Korean, Japanese, and Taiwanese products are available in many different forms in the West. Clothing, electronics, cars, toys, souvenirs, and thousands of other products are manufactured in the region and find their way to markets around the world.

East Asian cultures have long histories. Although they are deeply steeped in their traditional ways of life, trade, travel, and the media have brought a wave of new cultural aspects to the region. North Korea is quite isolated from these cultural currents, but the rest of the region is combining the richness of the past with new elements from abroad. At the same time, the people of East Asia are having a profound impact on the rest of the world because of their growing economic, political, and cultural strength.

CHAPTER 6

Governments in
East Asia

Governments in East Asia have varied and sometimes checkered pasts that range from cruel and violent dictatorships to strong and peaceful democracies. In the case of Japan, both of these types of government have existed within the past seven decades. Today, the East Asian neighborhood is still diverse in terms of the types and styles of governments; they range from North Korea's dictatorship to stable democracies in Japan, South Korea, and Taiwan. The governments of China and Mongolia appear to be in transition, although it is too early to determine what the outcomes will be. Governments are a reflection of a country's cultures and history. Countries (or their governments) are often in disagreement with one another, and relations can be extremely contentious. A prime example is the disagreements regarding

North Korea's quest for nuclear weapons, a factor that would greatly change the region's military geopolitics.

Other contentious issues include the continuing dialogue about Taiwan's status. China regards the country as a break-away province, but the island is trying to tiptoe its way toward political independence. Like the DMZ that separates North Korea and South Korea, the Taiwan Strait (or Formosa Strait), which separates Taiwan and mainland China, is heavily armed. Both sides are poised for war should the situation come to this. The issue of reunification is a hot topic, as it affects both China and Taiwan and North Korea and South Korea.

All of these issues spur interest in an examination of the political systems by which East Asia's countries are governed. This examination includes both the promises and actual practices that take place in regional governance. Constitutions in some cases are merely words on paper that are not put into practice. Human rights vary widely in practice, as do the roles of citizens. Some authoritarian regimes have developed virtual political cults that put leaders on a pedestal and make them almost god-like. Communism also flourishes in some nations; however, its personality has changed in places like China, where free-market (an economic market that operates with free competition) mechanisms have been successfully introduced, although under the watchful eye of the Communist Party. In Mongolia, the Communist Party remains strong, but it operates within a more democratic political environment.

CONSTITUTIONS

In most nations, a constitution represents the highest law. Its primary purpose is to establish the government and provide protections, freedoms, and rights for citizens. In democracies, the constitution is truly the highest law and the rule of law prevails over all individuals and political parties. This type of constitution provides for what is called the "rule of law" rather than the "rule of man." The rule of man means that some individuals operate above the law. A prime example of this is the rule of North Korea's Kim Jong Il. In his regime, he operates above the laws of North Korea. Thousands have been persecuted or repressed under his regime. This number includes members of his own family, as Kim's rule is often arbitrary, unequal, and unjust. Under the rule of man, life for citizens is precarious and uncertain. Opposition to the totalitarian leader is not possible without the threat of retaliation by torture, intimidation, or even death. With the rule of law, people are protected by the constitution and even the president and other leaders must obey the laws or suffer the consequences. In democracies, the constitution can protect citizens from the unjust actions of their government by protecting basic rights and freedoms.

The following chart describes basic government functions and identifies the institutions that are created by the constitutions of East Asia's six countries. Note that the constitutions are very recent, as all were created after World War II.

GOVERNMENTS
China

China's official name is the People's Republic of China (PRC). The country is a Communist state and has been since the takeover led by Mao Zedong in 1949, which resulted in the fall of Chiang Kai-shek and his Kuomintang Party (KMT). The KMT and Chiang fled to the island province of Taiwan, where they established the Republic of China (ROC) and claimed to be the rightful government of all of China.

Strangely, both China and Taiwan claim Dr. Sun Yat-sen as their historical political inspiration and forefather. Dr. Sun was a powerful political leader who had ties to both the Communist Party and the Kuomintang in the early twentieth century and tried to blend them into a unified force. He is known as the father of the Chinese Revolution, and he promoted the Three Principles of the People. Sun stressed nationalism, democracy, and socialism as key philosophical foundations. The Kuo-

KEY CONSTITUTIONAL GOVERNMENT PROVISIONS IN EAST ASIA

	China	Japan	North Korea	South Korea	Mongolia	Taiwan
Year of present constitution	1982	1947	1948*	1948	1992	1947
Head of state	President	Emperor	Chairman of the National Defense Commission	President	President	President
Head of government	Premier	Prime Minister	Premier	Premier	Prime Minister	Premier
Legislative branch	Unicameral	Bicameral	Unicameral	Unicameral	Unicameral	Unicameral
Names of house(s)	National People's Congress	Diet, Sangi-in and Shugi-in	Supreme People's Assembly	National Assembly	State Great Hural	Legislative Yuan
Highest court	Supreme People's Court	Supreme Court	Central Court	Supreme Court	Supreme Court	Judicial Yuan

* Significant revisions have taken place since the original constitution was created.

mintang claimed to be the legitimate heir of Sun's legacy, but it is true that the Communists also have a proper claim: Sun invited the Communists to participate in the governing process in a coalition with the Kuomintang.

After Sun's death in 1925, Chiang Kai-shek became the Kuomintang (also known as the Nationalists) leader. He continued Sun's work to unify the country, sometimes by force as smaller warlords resisted the move to bring the country together. He later turned against the Communists, and between 1927 and 1934 he mounted many campaigns designed to exterminate them. Mao Zedong and other Chinese Communist leaders resisted Chiang's forces. They undertook the 6,000-mile "Long March" in a retreat back to Shanxi Province, where they regrouped their troops.

A new element appeared with Japan's attacks on China. Both the Communists and the Nationalists fought the Japanese and defeated them in World War II with the help of Americans and other allies. The United States tried to foster a KMT and Communist coalition government just after the war. The effort quickly failed, and the two parties threw the nation into a civil war. In 1949, the Communists under Mao Zedong emerged victorious and the PRC was formed.

Today, the PRC claims to be composed of 23 provinces, with Taiwan as the twenty-third. Until the two entities are reunited, China actually has 22 provinces. The chief of state is the president, who is elected for a five-year term by the National People's Congress, as is the vice president. The president nominates a premier, who is ratified by the National People's Congress. The premier serves as the head of government.

The Communist Party dominates all of China's government, and only token minor parties are allowed to exist. These parties are under the strict control of the Communist Party, and little dissent is tolerated. The functions of the legislative branch are provided by the National People's Congress, and the Supreme People's Court serves as the highest court in China.

The Communist Party dominates all of China's government, and only token minor parties are allowed to exist. The functions of the legislative branch are provided by the National People's Congress (pictured), and the Supreme People's Court serves as the highest court in China.

Local people's congresses exist at the municipal, regional, and provincial levels, with local people's courts operating at the same levels. There are also specialized people's courts for military, maritime, and railway matters. Many written laws are still in development, as they were often derived from local customs and traditions.

Japan

Japan is a constitutional monarchy with a parliamentary form of government. The monarchy is represented by the emperor, and legend has it that these imperial roots trace back to Emperor Jimmu, who ruled in about 660 B.C. Japan's constitution went into effect in 1947, when it was imposed by the United States during the occupation after World War II. Inasmuch as the document was forced on Japan by a foreign power, it is surprising that the constitution has not been amended since then.

The country's legislature is called the Diet, and it is bicameral, meaning that it has two houses. These two bodies are the House of Councillors, or Kokkai, and the House of Representatives, or Shugi-in. The Kokkai has 252 members, who are elected for six-year terms. The Shugi-in has 480 members, who are elected for four-year terms. The emperor functions in a primarily ceremonial role; the true executive is the prime minister. This office is occupied by a member of the majority party or the majority coalition in the Diet. In contrast to China, with one dominant political party, Japan has many political parties. Parties often form coalitions in order to create the majority needed to form a government and elect a prime minister. Japan also has a minor Communist party called the Japan Communist Party (JCP), which normally receives enough votes to hold 4 to 8 percent of seats in the Diet.

Japan's highest court is the Supreme Court; it is modeled after similar courts in Europe and the United States. Other courts exist below the Supreme Court, which has the power to conduct judicial review of lower-court decisions. Fifteen judges serve on this court.

Political subdivisions in Japan include 47 districts called prefectures and more than 3,000 other local governments. These governments are responsible for safety, garbage collection, transportation, schools, and other issues best administered at the local level.

Mongolia

Landlocked Mongolia has a constitution that dates back to only 1992. Sandwiched between two huge superpowers—China and Russia—the country often served as a buffer between these two states. Mongolia has a strong Communist party called the Mongolian People's Revolutionary Party (MPRP) that has been in and out of power since the new constitution was adopted.

Mongolia has a unicameral legislature called the Great Hural. This body has 76 members who are elected by the people to four-year terms. The president is nominated by the political parties represented in the Great Hural and is elected by a direct vote of the people. The president, who serves as the chief of state, serves a four-year term with a two-term limit. Usually, the leader of the majority party in the Great Hural serves as prime minister and is responsible for heading the government.

The Supreme Court is the highest court in Mongolia. It has the power of judicial review of lower-court decisions, although it rarely reverses them. Other lower courts work with cases heard for the first time and for specialized matters like civil cases. Judges are nominated by the General Council for Courts and are approved by the president.

North Korea

The government of North Korea can be essentially summed up in one name: Kim Jong Il. This country has a totalitarian government under the iron-fist rule primarily of Kim. Kim took control in 1994, when his father, Kim Il Sung, died. North Korea's government is a virtual political cult with a dictatorship devoted to the public adoration of the dead leader Kim Il Sung and his son.

Given this context, the political institutions and rights afforded by the constitution are sometimes laughable. They are merely words and institutions that exist only at the pleasure of President Kim Jong Il. The constitution starts the charade of cult rule by stating in the preface, "The great leader Comrade Kim Il Sung is the sun of the nation and the lodestar of the reunification of the fatherland [South Korea]." Another passage in the preamble is filled with even more praise:

> Comrade Kim Il Sung was a genius ideological theoretician and a genius art leader, an ever-victorious, iron-willed brilliant commander, a great revolutionary and politician, and

The government of North Korea can be essentially summed up in one name: Kim Jong Il. Kim took control in 1994, when his father, Kim Il Sung, died. North Korea's government is a virtual political cult with a dictatorship devoted to the public adoration of the dead leader Kim Il Sung and his son.

a great human being. Comrade Kim Il Sung's great idea and achievements in leadership are the eternal treasures of the nation and a fundamental guarantee for the prosperity and efflorescence of the DPRK [Democratic People's Republic of Korea].

These passages are only a few of the 16 glowing descriptions of the leader's father found in the constitution. Democracies do not name individuals in their constitutions because the documents are more important than any one individual.

Government institutions in North Korea include the Supreme People's Assembly (SPA), which administers the functions of the legislative and judicial areas and meets only twice a year. The assembly is dominated by the Korean Workers Party (KWP) which is the North Korean Communist party. Decisions of the SPA simply rubber-stamp decisions made by the KWP and President Kim. All government workers are members of the KWP. The cabinet is called the State Administration Council, and it operates the ministries in the government. Other minor parties are allowed to exist, but only under tightly controlled and token circumstances.

The highest court in North Korea is the Central Court, but justice is limited in the country and freedoms are curtailed. Human rights are frequently violated, and freedom of expression is nonexistent for individuals and the media. The courts serve merely as puppets of the ruling regime, as rights given in the constitution are not protected. This problem is common in dictatorships. The rule of man prevails over the rule of law, and courts lack independence from the leadership, which can impose its own decisions.

South Korea

In stark contrast to North Korea, South Korea has developed democratic traditions in the era since the Korean War. Formally called the Republic of Korea (ROK), South Korea has a constitution that was originally adopted in 1948. Since the adoption, there have been revisions designed to protect individual rights and limit the president's powers. South Korea's constitution stands in sharp contrast to that of North Korea, with its numerous mentions of Kim Il Sung. In its preamble, South Korea's constitution begins with the phrase, "We, the people of Korea . . . . "

South Korea has a president, who is elected for a five-year term by a direct election of the people. The president can not be reelected and may serve only one term. Ministers are nominated by the prime minister and appointed by the president. The ministers serve as department heads and as advisors to the president.

The Republic of Korea has a unicameral legislature called the National Assembly. Members of the assembly are elected for four-year terms, and there must be at least 200 members in the assembly. No upper limit is set for membership. Political parties are often built around a strong individual rather than around a political philosophy. Regional conflicts are often present as a divisive force in elections and politics in general.

The highest court in South Korea is the Supreme Court. Justices are appointed by the president but must be approved by the National Assembly. They are appointed for six-year terms and may be reappointed. The chief justice is the lead judge on the Supreme Court and may serve a six-year term without the possibility of reappointment. The office of chief justice is a powerful position in that he or she appoints lower-court judges for ten-year terms. These appointments must be ratified by the Conference of Supreme Court Justices, and lower-court judges may be reappointed after serving a ten-year term.

Taiwan

China considers Taiwan a breakaway province, yet Taiwan operates as an independent entity with its own government, lead-

In March 2004, Taiwan held presidential elections. The incumbent president Chen Shuibian (right) and Vice President Annette Lu (left) greeted their supporters after winning the election and only one day after an assassination attempt in which both of them were wounded.

ers, and jurisdiction. The government of Taiwan is democratic, with a constitution that was first adopted in 1947. The document was amended four times in the 1990s in efforts to make government more democratic. The executive branch of Taiwan's government is headed by the president, who is elected, along with a vice president, for a term of four years. As in Mongolia, the president is the chief of state. The president appoints the premier, who serves as the head of the government.

Taiwan also has a one-house legislature called the Legislative Yuan. This body has an unusual process for selecting members. Of its 225 seats, 168 are filled by popular vote and 41 by a proportional vote of the island's political parties. Another eight are elected from overseas constituencies, and the final eight are elected by a vote of the island's aboriginal or native populations. Taiwan has many native tribes whose members qualify to run for office. Members serve terms of three years.

Taiwan has a second unicameral body called the National Assembly. This body meets rarely and has 300 members, who are nominated by the political parties and elected by proportional representation. The National Assembly meets only when called into session by the Legislative Yuan to act on issues of impeachment, to change the country's borders, or to amend the constitution.

The Judicial Yuan is the highest court in Taiwan. Members are appointed by the president, and the Legislative Yuan acts on the recommendations. Before 2003, the National Assembly approved court justices.

A controversial political issue in Taiwan is the subject of declaring independence from China. The long-held hope of reunification with mainland China and its Communist government is now openly questioned. The People's Republic of China looks very unfavorably on the issue of an independent Taiwan. This conflict has occasionally come close to military conflict, although to date military action has not been taken.

CITIZEN RIGHTS AND RESPONSIBILITIES

The role and importance of citizens vary widely in the region. Citizens in North Korea have many restrictions, even though certain rights may be protected in their countries' constitutions. China's constitution guarantees freedom of speech and the right to assemble and demonstrate. In 1989, however, the government forcefully put down popular demonstrations for democracy in Tiananmen Square. From this clash came an unforgettable image—that of a man standing defiantly in front of a tank in the square. This act provided an entire generation of people with a stark symbol of people trying to win the freedoms that the government had promised. Another example is Article 36 of China's constitution, which guarantees freedom of reli-

China's constitution guarantees freedom of speech and the right to assemble and demonstrate. In 1989, however, the government forcefully put down popular demonstrations for democracy in Tiananmen Square.

gion. In 1999, however, China's leadership began persecuting the Falungong spiritual movement. Since that time, thousands have been tortured or killed or have disappeared because of the continuing government action. Similar problems have occurred in North Korea.

Citizens also have responsibilities assigned by their constitutions. These duties also vary widely from country to country. In North Korea, citizens are required to take care of state property; no other country in the region has a similar provision. A strange duty appears in Article 85 of the North Korean constitution, which states, "Citizens shall constantly increase their revolutionary vigilance and devotedly fight for the security of the state." Loosely translated, this means that citizens have the responsibility of spying on other citizens to protect the state.

Throughout the region, citizens are required to defend the motherland or serve in the military if needed. Most citizens have a responsibility to work and pay taxes. Japan and South Korea require citizens to educate their children, and Mongolia requires citizens to protect nature and the environment. Only the Communist-led states—Mongolia, China, and North Korea—have provisions that require citizens to abide by the constitution and laws. This is in contrast to the three strong democracies in the region that do not have this constitutional duty. Most democracies recognize that arbitrary laws that require people to violate other laws may be created. For example, there can be laws that are morally wrong. This was true of many state laws in the American South during the era of racial segregation. Democracies in the region recognize that a way to protect democratic constitutions is for the people to remain vigilant. Morally wrong or unjust laws must be resisted and legally changed.

EAST ASIAN COUNTRIES AND FOREIGN RELATIONS

East Asian countries have become major economic powers. This, along with the huge population, helps make some East Asian countries important players on the international stage. China, for example, is one of only five countries with a permanent seat on the United Nations Security Council. This means that it—along with the United States, France, Russia, and the United Kingdom—has a veto power on Security Council resolutions. Japan, China, Mongolia, and the Republic of Korea have participated in international peacekeeping efforts. These four countries remain active in a variety of United Nations efforts.

Because of their unique political circumstances, North Korea and Taiwan are relatively isolated in international affairs. North Korea is isolated somewhat by choice. Its dismal internal political situation depends on secrecy and strong state control of the people, economy, and politics. North Korea uses this isolation to control its people and keep them from outside information and contact. North Korea also has made many enemies. It has a history of supplying advanced military weaponry to unsavory entities such as Burma (Myanmar), Iraq, and radical organizations. Today, the country also threatens to arm itself with nuclear weapons.

In contrast, the Republic of China (Taiwan) is isolated because the People's Republic of China demands international recognition as the only true China. Many countries, including the United States, have close relations with Taiwan but maintain official relations only with mainland China. This status means that Taiwan is not allowed to join the United Nations, the World Health Organization, and many other international organizations. Nonetheless, Taiwan would very much like to be admitted to these bodies as the Republic of China.

China, Japan, Mongolia, and the Koreas have chosen to participate in the Montreal Protocol, which commits them to phase out substances that cause ozone depletion. Excluding the Republic of China, all countries in the region also have signed the Kyoto Protocol, an initiative that strives to limit greenhouse gas emissions.

East Asia is a hotbed of economic activity. The trade among China, Japan, South Korea, Taiwan, and the rest of the world creates an influx of goods to the United States and other countries. Cheap labor in China has made its economy one of the world's fastest growing. Politics sometimes are injected into trade relationships as countries seek trade advantages with their customers and competitors. For example, China has been unwilling to increase the value of its currency. This makes their products inexpensive but has contributed to the United States's huge trade deficit with China. This issue also has strained American and Western relationships with Japan and South Korea in the recent past.

The political stability of governments in East Asia is a vital element in the region's continuing economic and political development. At the end of World War II, Japan lay in ruins and was emerging from a stifling dictatorship. It now has become one of the world's strongest democracies. Governments in South Korea and Taiwan became much more democratic during the 1990s. Mongolia has dabbled with democracy and seems to be moving more in that direction, although at an irregular pace. China has opened its economy, but political change has been slow. Will this economic change cause problems in the future as people gain more wealth and thereby create a middle class with higher democratic expectations? Will North Korea fall apart in an economic mess, fade away, unite with South Korea, or ignite this region and others in war? Many questions remain for the governments in this region of the world. The answers will affect not only the region, but the entire world.

CHAPTER 7

East Asian Economics

East Asia's countries run the gamut of economic systems and make a region of great economic contrast. At one extreme is the government-controlled economy of North Korea, which is a dismal failure. At the other end are the vibrant economy of Japan, which ranks third behind only the United States and the rapidly expanding economy of China. Sharp contrasts also exist in economic activities. Hundreds of millions of people live in the countryside and live in an agricultural economy relatively unchanged from that of their ancestors. At the same time, huge cities are modern in every way and teem with world-class industries, businesses, and services. Many such contrasts can be found in the same country and only a short distance from each other. Some countries are rich in natural resources, whereas others have few. Personal incomes in the region range from rich to impoverished, and access to technology varies from the world class to very primitive.

EAST ASIA ENTERS THE INDUSTRIAL AGE

Japan set much of the tone for economic development with the model it pursued after World War II. The country and its economy were devastated after the war, and it was occupied by Allied forces and thus was not allowed to govern itself. When the U.S. occupation ended in 1952, Japan started the difficult process of building a modern and advanced economy. With almost no natural resources and a rugged terrain that severely limits agriculture, it faced a huge task. A half-century ago, to consumers in the West, the label "Made in Japan" generally meant cheap goods of very low quality. Starting with toys, clothing, and other low-technology goods, the economy grew rapidly from the 1950s on, and by the late 1980s, the country's economy had grown to be the world's second largest. During the past several decades, "Made in Japan" has come to mean cars, electronics, robotics, and other goods of unsurpassed quality. All of this was achieved despite the country having to import about 97 percent of all natural resources and raw materials used in its industries!

How did Japan achieve this success? A major reason is the P-Q-R-S-T formula proposed by Dr. Charles F. Gritzner, a geographer at South Dakota State University. "P" refers to productivity and pride. Japanese workers take great pride in what they produce and have a high level of productivity during their work hours. "Q" stands for quality. Japanese cars and electronics are considered to be among the world's most reliable. "R" represents robotization. Japan is the world leader in robotics and has 410,000 of the world's 720,000 operating robots. This allows people to do more important tasks during work time. "S" stands for sales and savings. The Japanese people are among the world's leaders in their savings rate, and a personal touch is provided when they sell goods and services.

Japan continues to be a world leader in technology, with the greatest number of new patents issued, and has 410,000 of the world's 720,000 operating robots.

"T" refers to technology, an area where Japan, along with the United States, continues to be a world leader, with the greatest number of new patents issued. P-Q-R-S-T is a formula that many other nations in Asia have looked to as a model for successful economic development.

Other countries in the region, such as Taiwan, South Korea, and even China, to some extent, have followed Japan's post–World War II lead. Another key element in the rapid development of these economies has been the existence of governments that have allowed free-market systems to develop. These factors, coupled with government stability, have given a boost to many economies in East Asia, and this results in better-paying jobs for workers.

A REGION OF ECONOMIC CONTRASTS

In East Asia, economic contrasts can be very great within a country. Half of China's 1.3 billion people are still engaged in

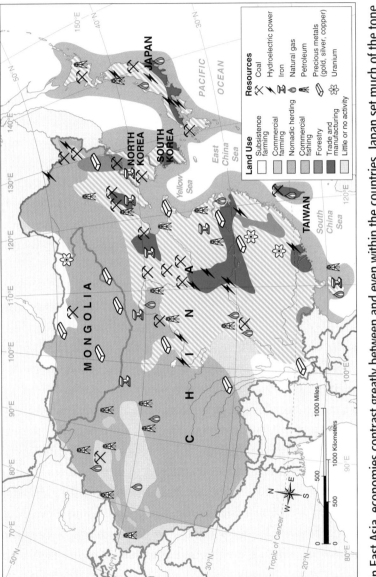

In East Asia, economies contrast greatly between and even within the countries. Japan set much of the tone for economic development with the model it pursued after World War II. Other countries in the region, such as Taiwan, South Korea, and even China, to some extent, have followed Japan's post–World War II lead. Meanwhile, half of China's 1.3 billion people are still engaged in agriculture.

agriculture. Most of the work is carried out with little modern equipment and by traditional farming methods on small plots of land. Contrast this with Shanghai, a bustling city that claims more than 20 million residents, 3 million of whom are "floaters," recent arrivals from rural areas. The city also will have the world's tallest building in 2007, when the Shanghai World Financial Center is completed.

The height of Asia's skyscrapers seems to reflect the heights that their economies are reaching. At the turn of the millennium, the world's tallest buildings were the Petronas Towers in Kuala Lumpur, Malaysia (in Southeast Asia), at 1,483 feet (452 meters). Taiwan seized the mantle in 2003 with the Taipei 101 building, which reaches 1,676 feet (511 meters) skyward. China, alone, has three other buildings that are nearly one-quarter of a mile (.4 kilometer) tall. The country's economy is rising nearly as fast as the skyscrapers, with annual growth rates that have approached 10 percent in recent years.

In marked contrast to the dynamic economies of China, Japan, South Korea, and Taiwan stands that of North Korea. Saddled with a repressive government, the economy has had little success in moving forward. The country spends much of its income on military hardware and personnel. As a result, hunger, malnutrition, and poverty have gripped the country for more than a decade. The government's centrally planned economy makes the problem worse. In 2004, for example, international food aid from the World Food Programme, Russia, the United States, and others was offered to North Korea. It was sometimes blocked by the government of Kim Jong Il, who would not accept that his policies had failed. Some food aid is believed to have been redirected to the military. Today, the economy of North Korea remains in shambles and stands in stark contrast to prosperity enjoyed elsewhere in the region.

MEASURES OF ECONOMIC DEVELOPMENT

One of the important considerations in measuring economies is the gross domestic product (GDP). This is the total amount of goods and services produced in a country during a year. Another measure is purchasing power parity (PPP), which refers to the amount that a person can buy, because prices and incomes vary in different countries. Purchasing power parity allows researchers to accurately compare data among countries. The chart on the next page shows key economic indicators for the countries of East Asia.

Note that the numbers of North Korea and Mongolia contrast with those of the other countries. Per capita GDP ranges from the low of $1,000 in North Korea to a high of $28,700 in Japan. This rate is increasing in most of these economies but much more slowly in the economies dominated by agriculture. The rate in China has experienced a meteoric increase. In 1989, the per capita GDP was $360; in 2004, it had soared to $4,700, a twelve-fold increase! The implications of China becoming a consumer society are huge for the world's economy and environment. Some observers predict that China will soon surpass the United States in terms of GDP. This is somewhat misleading because China has more than four times the population of the United States; thus, the per capita GDP of the United States will remain much higher for the foreseeable future. Still, China's rapid economic ascent will have numerous consequences for the world's economy, politics, and environment.

REGIONAL ECONOMIES

The following section provides a snapshot of the economies of each country in East Asia. For each, there is a glimpse of the range of economic activities, their economic potential, and the resource base.

China

The People's Republic of China is one of the great economic success stories of recent decades. Its development has been marked by the amazing transition from a largely subsistence-agriculture economy to a modern industrial economy with a rapidly growing service sector. Since the 1970s, China has

SELECTED EAST ASIAN ECONOMIC DATA (2004 ESTIMATE)

	GDP (PPP)	GDP by Sector	GDP Per Capita (PPP)	GDP Growth Rate	Labor Force	Unemployment Rate	Currency
China	$5.989 trillion	Ag. 15.2% Ind. 51.2% Ser. 33.6%	$4,700	8%	Ag. 50% Ind. 22% Ser. 28%	10% (est)	Yuan
Japan	$3.651 trillion	Ag. 1.4% Ind. 30.9% Ser. 67.7%	$28,700	0.2%	Ag. 5% Ind. 22% Ser. 28%	5.4%	Yen
Mongolia	$5.06 billion	Ag. 32% Ind. 23% Ser. 45%	$1,900	3.9%	Herding and agriculture	20%	Tughrik
North Korea	$22.6 billion	Ag. 30.4% Ind. 32.3% Ser. 37.3%	$1,000	1%	Ag. 36% Nonag. 64%	N/A	North Korean Won
South Korea	$941 billion	Ag. 4.4% Ind. 41.6% Ser. 54%	$19,600	6.3%	Ag. 9.5% Ind. 21.5% Ser. 69%	3.1%	South Korean Won
Taiwan	$406 billion	Ag. 2% Ind. 31% Ser. 67%	$18,000	3.5%	Ag. 7% Ind. 35% Ser. 58%	5.2%	New Taiwan Dollar

Ag., agriculture; est., estimated; Ind., industry; Nonag., nonagriculture; Ser., services

This is Shanghai's new financial center. Since the 1970s, China has grown from being a relatively impoverished nation to having the world's second-ranking GDP.

grown from being a relatively impoverished nation to having the world's second-ranking GDP. Today, it is crossing new economic frontiers, taking major steps toward developing an aerospace industry. In October 2003, Chinese astronaut Yang Liwei orbited the earth 14 times and safely returned. This event placed China in an exclusive club with only the United States and Russia. China's leaders called the event the fulfillment of a millennial dream, and the world viewed China with new eyes at the beginning of the third millennium.

China's entrance onto the world's economic stage is viewed with both respect and fear by other countries. The country has a huge natural resource base, with oil, coal, iron, tin, and other essential materials necessary for economic development. It also has a huge labor force that is paid relatively low salaries when compared with other developed countries. Starting in 1978, with the Four Modernizations (agriculture, industry, science, and technology) plan promoted by Premier Deng Xiaoping, China's economy began to take major steps forward. Prior to the implementation of this plan, the economy had been centrally planned by the government. This policy change by the Communist government allowed for the gradual development of free-market mechanisms. These changes in policy have pushed the economy forward at a sometimes staggering rate.

Also with these changes, the gap in income between the rich and poor and urban and rural areas became larger. Migration to China's cities now threatens to choke the country's urban centers with an additional 12 million people per year for the foreseeable future. New roads, housing, water, sewage, and other urban infrastructures will be necessary to satisfy the needs of the new immigrants. Failure to keep up with this urbanization will ultimately have a negative impact on the economy and on quality of life.

Increased consumerism in China is an important matter for the entire world. With its huge population, the country is the world's largest consumer market. In the past, lack of financial resources kept most Chinese from becoming too consumer oriented. Now, newly rich Chinese have expensive cars and homes filled with luxuries of which they only could have dreamed in the past. The cumulative impact of China as a consumer society can be staggering to the world's economy and environment. China is already the second-largest consumer of oil with demand increasing daily. A decade ago, this country was an oil exporter; now it is an importer. China may also soon become an importer of coal to help fuel its industries. Presently, coal provides about 70 percent of China's energy. China does have a wealth of hydroelectric potential, including the current development with the Three Gorges Dam scheduled for completion in 2009. Certainly, the future will see tremendous growth in the country's thirst for energy.

Environmental degradation is a mounting concern as China turns toward a consumer economy. Economic growth is combined with a general lack of public policy to regulate pollution and factors that diminish environmental quality. Major air pollution problems exist in Chinese cities, primarily because of coal-generated power. Adding to this dilemma is pollution caused by a rapid increase in motor vehicle ownership. Other challenges that face China are water pollution and shortages in some areas of the country, along with deforestation and desertification (creation of desert conditions by human activity).

Japan

Japan's entry into the twenty-first century was a bit confusing economically, as the economy had stagnated during the 1990s. During recent years, Japan's GDP has been surpassed by that of China, dropping the country to third place among the world's nations. The Nikkei stock index dropped from a high of nearly 39,000 in 1989 to barely more than 14,000 in less than three years. Stocks and land had been greatly overvalued by the late 1980s, and both fell sharply in value during the 1990s. By mid-2005, Japan's stock market and the Nikkei still had not recovered—the index rested at less than 12,000.

Another major factor that affected Japan during this time was the problem of deflation. With inflation, prices of goods increase. With deflation, prices drop. This sounds good for the consumer, but it means that companies earn less, wages may decrease, and people spend less. This can create a deflation cycle that takes a country backward in terms of economic development. This problem has faced Japan since the early 1990s.

During recent years, under new political leadership, Japan's economy has shown signs of reigniting. The government has begun to take new and bold steps to move the economy forward. By 2003, not only was the economy on a growth curve, but for the first time in 13 years it briefly once again exceeded the growth rate in the United States.

Issues remain for the country and its constant need to import natural resources from other countries. Because of this need, combined with its huge industrial output, Japan is a leader in terms of world trade. It has succeeded by importing energy and other natural resources and then producing high-quality products that are sold domestically and exported. The United States is Japan's leading trading partner, buying nearly 30 percent of its exports. The United States is followed by China (9.6 percent), South Korea (6.9 percent), and Taiwan (6.2 percent).

Japan's imports primarily come from China, the United States, South Korea, Indonesia, and Australia. Top imports include machinery and equipment, fuels, foodstuffs, chemicals, textiles, and raw materials. In recent years, Japan exported about 100 billion U.S. dollars more than it imported. This figure alone is more than four times the entire GDP of North Korea.

Even with the difficulties in Japan's economy during recent years, productivity of the country's work force has remained high. The country's impact on the global economy is great, as Japanese trade reaches to all corners of the world. Its transportation and communication systems are first class in every respect and operate with exceptional efficiency.

Problems that remain for Japan's economy include many environmental obstacles. Volcanoes, earthquakes, landslides, and even tsunamis can take a severe economic and human toll. Government bureaucracy, increasing indebtedness, and occasional scandals caused by corruption have also plagued the country's recent efforts to reform the economy. A final challenge for the economy is much-needed reform of the banking industry that holds billions of yen in bad loans.

Mongolia

The economy of Mongolia is still mostly agrarian (agricultural). Primary products include wheat, barley, potatoes, and forage crops. With vast steppe grasslands, grazing is very important; herds of sheep, goats, cattle, camels, and horses are typical sights

The steppes (vast, treeless plains) of Mongolia support a mostly agrarian (agricultural) economy. Mongolia also has a valuable natural resource base, with copper, coal, molybdenum, tin, tungsten, and gold deposits.

on the country's expansive landscape. Mongolia also has a valuable natural resource base, with copper, coal, molybdenum, tin, tungsten, and gold deposits. Unfortunately, this country is entirely dependent on others for oil, a factor that throws its economy into a tailspin when oil prices increase rapidly.

Because Mongolia is landlocked, trade is difficult: The lack of harbors denies it a major gateway to the world for exportation and importation. This factor makes it easy to understand why Mongolia imports primarily from its neighbors, Russia (32 percent) and China (19.4 percent). Exports mainly go to China (43.8 percent), the United States (33.6 percent), and Russia (9.6 percent).

In the 1980s, Mongolia received huge amounts of assistance from the Soviet Union. Often as much as one-third of the country's GDP (much in the form of oil) was Soviet aid. With the fall of the Soviet Union, the assistance stopped and Mongolia's economy crashed. In response, the government has instituted many free-market reforms that have helped create a more dynamic economy. This has raised the country's GDP. A continuing problem is the high level of foreign debt that Mongolia has with Russia and other countries. This debt is a major drag on the economy.

North Korea

South Korea has prospered during the half century since the Korean War, but the economy of North Korea has virtually stagnated. Machinery is worn out, and the infrastructure (highways, railroads, and airports) has declined in quality. Systems have fallen apart because of lack of repair and lack of new capital spending. Military expenditures account for more than one-third of North Korea's GDP; the nation has pushed hard to develop nuclear weapons and rocket delivery systems. This, combined with an economy centrally controlled by the authoritarian government, has left the people of North Korea with a precarious life. Hunger and malnutrition are widespread, and the country has one of the world's lowest per capita GDP rates.

Exports by North Korea are very limited and amount to less than U.S. one billion dollars per year. Much of the country's exportation is in the unsavory trade of military weaponry to other questionable regimes, some of which promote terrorism. Primary imports include oil, grains, machinery, and textiles from China, Brazil, and India.

Starting in 2003, North Korea has made new efforts to obtain hard currencies. At the same time, however, it refuses to relinquish the tight-fisted government control over the economy. There has been limited success with some European investors, but there are many roadblocks, in part because of a strong international mistrust of North Korea's dictatorial leadership. Poor government, a closed market, and widespread poverty all serve to discourage investment and economic improvement in the foreseeable future.

South Korea

Early in 2004, South Korean scientists announced that they were the first in the world to successfully clone a human embryo. This process is extremely controversial, but it demonstrates the high level of capability that now exists in South Korea.

South Korea is one of the "Four Tigers"; the others are Taiwan, Hong Kong (now part of China), and Singapore. Following much of the Japanese P-Q-R-S-T model, the economy has bolted upward at an amazing pace. During recent decades, the country's annual GDP has grown at rates near, reaching, or surpassing 10 percent. In the 1970s, South Koreans had a standard of living comparable to those of many of the world's poorer nations. Today, its per capita GDP is higher than those of such countries as Israel, Portugal, Greece, and several other developed nations. With high productivity, rising incomes, and the quality of life improving, the government reduced the work week from six days to five in 2003.

South Korea is also a leading nation in terms of international trade, ranking twelfth in terms of exports. Exports include electronics, cars, shoes, steel, machinery, ships, and clothing, among others. Recipients of South Korea's products in order include the United States (20.4 percent), China (14.7 percent), Japan (9.4 percent), and Hong Kong (6.3 percent). The country is the fifteenth-leading importer of foreign goods and receives mostly machinery, electronics, oil, chemicals, and grain. The main countries that South Korea depends on for imports are Japan (19.6 percent), the United States (15.2 percent), China (11.4 percent), and Saudi Arabia (5 percent).

Taiwan

Another member of the Four Tigers is the island of Taiwan. Taiwan's economy has a dynamic free-market system that has successfully undergone a transition from agriculture to a service- and industry-based economy during the past 50 years. An example of its rapid growth is GDP: Taiwan's has grown at the incredible annual average rate of 8 percent for the past 30 years.

Taiwan holds large reserves of other currencies and ranks third in the world in this area. These foreign reserves are the result of huge trade surpluses that have accumulated. With this cash, Taiwan has become an important investor in many other Asian countries. Major exports include machinery, electrical equipment, metals, textiles, plastics, and chemicals. Hong Kong (23.9 percent), the United States (20.8 percent), Japan (9.3 percent), and China (7.7 percent) are the primary recipients of Taiwanese goods. Imports come mainly from Japan (24.3 percent), the United States (16.1 percent), China (7.1 percent), and South Korea (6.9 percent).

Like Japan, Taiwan has limited natural resources, but its location on the Pacific Rim has allowed it to connect with the world. Present plans include one to make Taiwan a hub for container traffic in the region, a goal that is spurring renovations to Taiwan's major ports.

EAST ASIA AND THE GLOBAL ECONOMY

The economies of East Asia touch families around the world every day. Most Americans and Canadians have tens of thousands of dollars of products from that region in their homes. These items include cars, CD players and speakers, computer equipment, and communications equipment. Most homes also have coffeemakers, can openers, cameras, watches, lamps, clothing, toys, games, and hundreds of other items of East Asian manufacture. Take a few moments to look around your house and note where different items were made. The majority in most homes are from East Asia.

With its rapid economic expansion and emergence as an international economic power, China remains a country to watch. Already a huge influence on the economies of Southeast and East Asia, the country is now connected with most of the world. If its growth trend continues, China will soon surpass the United States as the world's largest economy. How China chooses to use this new economic power is of profound importance to the rest of the world.

With some of the world's leading economies in East Asia and most leading nations located along the rim of the Pacific Ocean—a modern-day sea link to the world—the future looks promising for free-market economies. The P-Q-R-S-T model implemented by Japan has been used as a reference point by South Korea, Taiwan, China, and many other Asian countries. This successful model has moved countries in the region to new levels of productivity and economic success. Four of the countries in East Asia are economic success stories: China, Japan, South Korea, and Taiwan are modern societies with strong economies. Mongolia is in transition from a Soviet-style planned economy to a free-market system. The results in recent years have been promising for the country. North Korea has the most on the negative side. The current leadership and centrally controlled economy may lead to self-destruction and disintegration in the manner of the former Soviet Union. North Korea might also begin to see the opportunity provided by capitalist systems with much less government control. On the whole, East Asia is emerging as the world's most dynamic economic region, and its future looks bright.

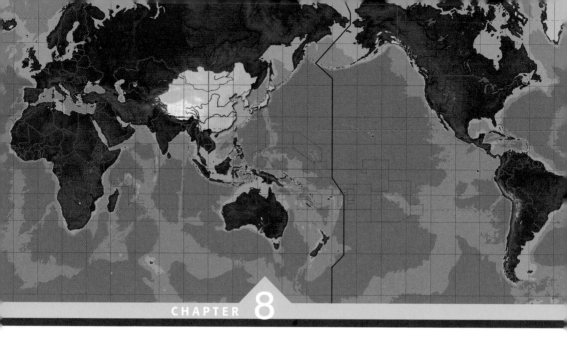

CHAPTER 8

East Asia Looks Ahead

In March 2004, Taiwan held presidential elections. The level of anticipation was very high, as a reform-minded incumbent named Chen Shui-bian was running for reelection. Chen and his Democratic Progressive Party were taking steps toward nationhood and permanent division from China. The KMT candidate, Lien Chan, and others in Taiwan feared that this would bring war with the mainland.

The day before the election on March 20, there was an assassination attempt on Chen and Vice President Annette Lu in the southern city of Tainan. Both were shot. Fortunately, neither was badly hurt and the elections were held as scheduled. The citizens of Taiwan were in shock, because violence is rare in that society. To make matters even more challenging, the race was extremely close. What were the results? That will come later.

The twenty-first century has been referred to as the "Century of the Pacific" by Mike Mansfield, former U.S. ambassador to Japan. This is true in many ways—population, world economy, technology, and in other areas.

Unexpected things can and often do quickly change the course of history. Predicting the future of East Asia is impossible; a mere bullet can change the course of events in a fraction of a second. With a long history of conflict in the region, the future may be as precarious as the past has been. The future might also be filled with peace and prosperity. When attempting to look ahead, it is always useful to examine past and ongoing trends and patterns that occur in a region.

By peering into the future, demographers provide some information that can be useful. Population trends in the region are revealing: China's population is projected to grow to a whopping 1.45 billion by the year 2025. Following projections, by 2050 it will drop to about 1.39 billion, an amazing turn of events. Population is expected to decline in Japan, Taiwan, and South Korea between 2025 and 2050, as deaths begin to surpass births in number. Only Mongolia has significant increases projected through 2050. North Korea's population is predicted to remain about the same.

China's growth in the coming two decades presents issues that will directly affect the rest of the world. The rising demand for oil and consumer goods affects the rest of the world as oil prices climb steadily higher. Some project that the world's oil production will begin to decline by 2010, if not before. With increasing demand for energy from China, India, and other countries, prices will rise until alternate energy sources become more viable.

China's increasing prosperity, a result of its rapid economic development, is also projected to continue. This will make China a powerful player in shaping world events. Will the power be used to exert greater control over neighbors in the region? Will the country rise to challenge the West and the United States? Will the new prosperity be used to increase military strength or for improving the status of citizens? Citizens have little freedom of expression in this Communist-ruled country. Even technology such as instant messaging is policed by the government. It keeps a watchful eye on people who might use the technology to incite resistance and demonstrations against the government. Although economic progress has been great for China, there has been little progress in democratizing the country since the demonstrations in Tiananmen Square in 1989. An important lingering question about China is whether the people will continue to accept economic advancement without an increase in political freedoms.

Japan, Taiwan, and South Korea most likely will continue to have strong economies. Japan's economy slumped during most of the 1990s, but during recent years, it has become more robust and shows signs of continuing growth. The quality of products from these countries is excellent, and brand names from the region represent some of the world's best consumer values.

With most East Asian countries lying on the Pacific Ocean, continuing economic strength is projected. Trade opportunities are enhanced by access to the sea that provides all but Mongolia with a window to world markets. Free and open sea lanes must be maintained to ensure continued development. The threat of piracy has increased in the region as oil tankers and container ships have become targets for thieves and terrorists. Oil traveling to East Asia from the Middle East is often transported through the strategic Strait of Malacca, south of Singapore and Malaysia. The sinking of a ship in the strait could block the passage and greatly disrupt world trade.

Regional conflicts with long-standing histories remain as explosive issues. The divide between North Korea and South Korea is still great because North Korea threatens to bring nuclear

The divide between North Korea and South Korea is still great because North Korea threatens to bring nuclear weapons to the peninsula. With thousands of violations of the DMZ rules by North Korea, South Korea stands ready to resist an invasion that could take place in only a few minutes.

weapons to the peninsula. Some believe that this quest for nuclear weapons is a tool to blackmail South Korea, the United States, and others into providing food for North Korea's people. Others believe that it gives North Korea a lingering threat to use against South Korea. The nuclear threat also poses a major problem for Japan, as the scars of animosity between the Koreans and Japanese linger. With thousands of violations of the DMZ rules by North Korea, South Korea stands ready to resist an invasion that could take place in only a few minutes. Air raid drills often quiet the streets of Seoul as people practice for a possible air attack by North Korea. South Korea has worked to build ties with North Korea and has conducted family exchanges in efforts to decrease tension on the peninsula. With all of this, the fate of the Koreas could take many unforeseen turns in coming years.

The relationship between Taiwan and China also remains tenuous. The 2004 assassination attempt and narrow reelection of President Chen Shui-bian in Taiwan has stretched the division between the two even more. Most do not believe that the Chinese government was behind the assassination, but rumors persist and fuel the continued division. China is extremely wary of Chen's leadership and his talk about a new constitution in 2008. China threatens that it will never allow Taiwan to become independent. In the summer of 2004, in fact, China's military chief, Jiang Zemin, vowed to annex the island by 2020. Jiang's comment came at a time when thousands of Chinese troops were practicing a military invasion of Taiwan in Taiwan Strait. This conflict is perhaps the most dangerous in the region. The two Chinese entities have strong militaries, and a PRC invasion of the island would directly involve the United States. The consequences of such a war are frightening to consider.

This leisurely cruise though East Asia has taken you on a course through the geography of this important region. The journey has featured both smooth and rough waters for these countries. The past is prologue, and the future holds both negative and positive possibilities. If conflict can be avoided in the Koreas and between China and Taiwan, the future seems exceedingly bright. Well-educated populations provide a continuing base for economic development and prosperity. Democratic reforms in North Korea and China could promote even further cooperation and development. Most countries in the world are closely linked to this region, most commonly through trade and goods. It is clear, therefore, that the world will watch closely to see how the future unfolds in East Asia. We all hope for smooth sailing.

900,000– **130,000-00 B.C.**	Peking Man lives near Beijing.
300,000	The first humans arrive on the Korean Peninsula.
30,000	The first settlers arrive in Japan.
12,000–2,000	The Neolithic period occurs in China.
10,000	The Joman, a nomadic people, settle in Japan.
6000	The Bronze Age begins in China.
2000–1500	The Xia Dynasty rules in China.
1700–1027	The Shang Dynasty rules in China.
1200–900	Rice is introduced into Korea from China.
1027–221	The Western Zhou Dynasty rules in China.
551	Confucius is born in China.
300	The Yayoi people replace the Joman and introduce agriculture.
206 B.C.– **A.D.220**	The Han Dynasty rules in China.
57 B.C.– **A.D. 668**	The Three Kingdoms exist in Korea.
265–420	The Eastern and Western Jin Dynasties rule in China.
300–710	The Kofun and Asuka era dominates in Japan; the Chinese written language is introduced.
581–617	The Sui Dynasty rules in China.
618–907	The Tang Dynasty rules in China.
668–935	The Unified Silla Dynasty exists in Korea.
710–794	The Nara period exists in Japan.
794–1185	The Heian period exists in Japan.
918–1392	The Koryo Dynasty exists in Korea.
960–1279	The Song Dynasty rules in China.
1162	Genghis Khan is born in Mongolia.
1185–1333	The Kamakura period exists in Japan.
1274–1281	The Mongols under Kublai Khan try and fail to invade Japan.
1279–1368	The Yuan Dynasty rules in China.

1292	Kublai Khan (Genghis Kan's grandson) dies.
1350	Mongol rule and power begins to decline.
1368–1644	The Ming Dynasty rules in China.
1392–1910	The kingdom of Chosun exists in Korea.
1543	The Portuguese arrive in Japan and bring trade, guns, and Christianity.
1544	The Portuguese land on Taiwan and call it Ilha Formosa, which means beautiful island.
1600–1868	The Tokugawa period exists in Japan; the capital is moved to Edo (Tokyo).
1639	Japan closes its doors to the outside world.
1644–1911	The Qing Dynasty rules in China.
1683	The Qing Dynasty of China conquers Taiwan.
1732–1911	Mongolia is under the rule of the Chinese dynasties.
1853	Commodore Matthew C. Perry arrives in Tokyo Harbor and opens Japan.
1868–1912	The Meiji Restoration takes place in Japan.
1890	The last samurai uprising occurs in Japan.
1894–1895	Japan defeats China in the Sino-Japanese War; after the war, Taiwan is ceded to Japan by China.
1895–1945	Taiwan is under Japanese control.
1904–1905	Japan wins the Russo-Japanese War.
1911	Mongolia becomes independent from China.
1911–1949	The Republic of China exists on the mainland.
1912	Japan annexes Korea.
1926	Emperor Hirohito assumes the throne in Japan.
1931	Japan seizes Manchuria.
1937–1945	The second Sino-Japanese War takes place.
1941	Japan attacks Pearl Harbor, the Philippines, and Singapore.

1945 Japan surrenders at end of World War II; the United States drops atomic bombs on the cities of Hiroshima and Nagasaki; Mongolia and the Soviet Union declare war on Japan in the last days of World War II.

1946 All Japanese are expelled from Taiwan.

1945–1949 A Chinese civil war, between the Communists and the KMT, takes place.

1949 The People's Republic of China is established on the mainland by Communists; the Republic of China is established on Taiwan by the Nationalists as more than one million of Chiang Kai-shek's followers flee to the island.

1950 North Korea invades South Korea.

1950–1953 The Korean War takes place.

1952 The U.S. occupation of Japan ends.

1956 Japan becomes a member of the United Nations.

1960 Mongolia sides with the Soviet Union during its split with China.

1961 Mongolia becomes a member of the United Nations.

1964 Tokyo hosts the Summer Olympics.

1966–1976 The Cultural Revolution takes place in China.

1968 North Korea signs the Nuclear Non-Proliferation Treaty.

1971 Chiang Kai-shek's Republic of China is removed from the United Nations.

1972 U.S. President Richard Nixon makes a historic trip to China; Sapporo, Japan, hosts the Winter Olympics.

1975 Chiang Kai-shek dies; his son, Chiang Ching-kuo, assumes leadership.

1976 Mao Zedong dies.

1989 Mongolia establishes diplomatic relations with China.

1990 The first democratically elected Great Hural meets in Mongolia.

1991 North Korea and South Korea join the United Nations.

1992 Mongolia's new constitution takes effect.

1993 The first presidential election takes place in Mongolia.

1994 North Korea's leader, Kim Il Sung, dies.

1997 Kim Jong Il assumes the position of general secretary in North Korea.

1998 Nagano, Japan, hosts the Winter Olympics; North Korea tests a rocket over Japan.

2000 Leaders of North Korea and South Korea meet for the first time.

2001 China joins the World Trade Organization.

2002–2003 The SARS outbreak occurs in China; North Korea announces its intent to withdraw from the Nuclear Non-Proliferation Treaty and that it possesses nuclear weapons.

2004 There is a preelection assassination attempt on ROC President Chen Shui-bian and Vice-President Annette Lu.

2008 China to host the Summer Olympics.

Barnes, Gina L. *China Korea and Japan: The Rise of Civilization in East Asia.* London: Thames & Hudson, 1993.

Berger, Mark T., and Douglas A. Borer. *The Rise of East Asia: Critical Visions of the Pacific Century.* London and New York: Routledge, 1997.

Cohen, Warren I. *East Asia at the Center.* New York: Columbia University Press, 2001.

Copper, John Franklin. *Taiwan: Nation–State or Province?* (Nations of the Modern World: Asia). Boulder, CO: Westview Press, 1996.

Gascoigne, Bamber, and Christina Gascoigne. *The Dynasties of China: A History.* New York: Carrol & Graf Publishers, 2003.

Gibney, Frank, *The Pacific Century: American and Asia in a Changing World.* New York: Macmillan Publishing Company, 1992.

Gritzner, Charles F., Douglas A. Phillips, and Kristi L. Desaulniers. *Japan (Modern World Nations).* Philadelphia: Chelsea House Publishers, 2004.

Kalman, Bobbie. *China: The Culture.* New York: Crabtree Publishing Company, 2001.

Lee, Kenneth B. *Korea and East Asia: The Story of a Phoenix.* Westport, CT: Praeger Publishers, 1997.

Miller, Debra A. *North Korea* (History of Nations). Detroit: Greenhaven Press, 2003.

Murphey, Rhoads. *East Asia: A New History,* 3rd edition. New York: Longman, 2003.

Naff, Clay Farris. *Japan (History of Nations).* Detroit: Greenhaven Press, 2004.

Nash, Amy K. *North Korea (Places and Peoples of the World).* Philadelphia: Chelsea House Publishers, 1991.

Netzley, Patricia D. *Japan (Modern Nations of the World).* Detroit: Greenhaven Press, 2000.

Oberdorfer, Don. *The Two Koreas: A Contemporary History, (Revised and updated edition).* New York: Basic Books, 2002.

Phillips, Douglas A., and Steven C. Levi. *The Pacific Rim Region: Emerging Giant.* Hillside, NJ: Enslow Publishers, Inc., 1988.

Salter, Christopher. *North Korea* (Modern World Nations). Philadelphia: Chelsea House Publishers, 2003.

Salter, Christopher L. *South Korea (Modern World Nations)*. Philadelphia: Chelsea House Publishers, 2005.

Salter, Christopher L. *Taiwan (Modern World Nations)*. Philadelphia: Chelsea House Publishers, 2004.

Shirokauer, Conrad, and Donald Clark. *Modern East Asia: A Brief History.* Belmont, CA: Thomson Wadsworth, 2004.

Weightman, Barbara A. *Dragons and Tigers: A Geography of South, East, and Southeast Asia,* updated edition. New York: John Wiley & Sons, 2004

Whiteford, Gary T. *China (Modern World Nations)*. Philadelphia: Chelsea House Publishers, 2002.

BOOKS

Barnes, Gina L. *China Korea and Japan: The Rise of Civilization in East Asia.* London: Thames & Hudson, 1993.

Berger, Mark T. and Douglas A. Borer. *The Rise of East Asia: Critical Visions of the Pacific Century.* London and New York: Routledge, 1997.

Cohen, Warren I. *East Asia at the Center.* New York: Columbia University Press, 2001.

Copper, John Franklin. *Taiwan: Nation-State or Province? (Nations of the Modern World: Asia).* Boulder, CO: Westview Press, 1996.

Gascoigne, Bamber and Christina Gascoigne. *The Dynasties of China: A History.* New York: Carrol & Graf Publishers, 2003.

Gritzner, Charles F. Douglas A. Phillips and Kristi L. Desaulniers. *Japan (Modern World Nations).* Philadelphia: Chelsea House Publishers, 2004.

Green, Robert. *China (Modern Nations of the World).* San Diego, CA: Lucent Books, 1999.

Kalman, Bobbie. *China: The Culture.* New York: Crabtree Publishing Company, 2001.

Lee, Kenneth B. *Korea and East Asia: The Story of a Phoenix.* Westport, CT: Praeger Publishers, 1997.

Leeming, Frank. *The Changing Geography of China (Studies in Geography).* Oxford, UK: Blackwell Publishers, 1993.

Liu, Fu-Kuo, and Philippe Regnier. *Regionalism in East Asia.* London and New York: Routledge/Curzon, 2002.

Miller, Debra A. *North Korea (History of Nations).* Detroit: Greenhaven Press, 2003.

Murphey, Rhoads. *East Asia: A New History,* 3rd edition. New York: Longman, 2003.

Naff, Clay Farris. *Japan (History of Nations).* Detroit: Greenhaven Press, 2004.

Nash, Amy K. *North Korea (Places and Peoples of the World).* Philadelphia: Chelsea House Publishers, 1991.

Netzley, Patricia D. *Japan (Modern Nations of the World).* Detroit: Greenhaven Press, 2000.

Oberdorfer, Don. *The Two Koreas: A Contemporary History (revised and updated edition)*. New York: Basic Books, 2002.

Ogden Suzanne, *Global Studies: China*. New York: McGraw-Hill/Dushkin, 2005.

Palka, Eugene J., and Francis Galgano, Jr. *North Korea: Geographic Perspectives*. New York: McGraw-Hill/Dushkin, 2003.

Phillips, Douglas A., and Steven C. Levi. *The Pacific Rim Region: Emerging Giant*. Hillside, NJ: Enslow Publishers, Inc. 1988.

Salter, Christopher. *North Korea (Modern World Nations)*. Philadelphia: Chelsea House Publishers, 2003.

Salter, Christopher L. *South Korea (Modern World Nations)*. Philadelphia: Chelsea House Publishers, 2005.

Salter, Christopher L. *Taiwan (Modern World Nations)*. Philadelphia: Chelsea House Publishers, 2004.

Schirokauer, Conrad and Donald Clark. *Modern East Asia: A Brief History*. Belmont, CA: Thomson Wadsworth, 2004.

Weightman, Barbara A. *Dragons and Tigers: A Geography of South, East, and Southeast Asia, updated edition*. New York: John Wiley & Sons, 2005.

Whiteford, Gary T. *China (Modern World Nations)*. Philadelphia: Chelsea House Publishers, 2002.

Williams, Jean K. *South Korea (Modern Nations of the World)*. San Diego, CA: Lucent Books, 1999.

WEBSITES

About.com
http://geography.about.com/

This site provides an assortment of geographic perspectives with East Asian connections.

Access Asia, Australian Asian Education Foundation
http://www.curriculum.edu.au/accessasia/

This site provides general information, curriculum resources, and materials on China, Japan, and Korea.

Asia Society
http://www.asiasociety.org

This Web site features aspects of Asian culture and society.

CNN's Talk Asia
http://edition.cnn.com/ASIA/talkasia/
CNN's site provides current events in Asia, combining articles from CNN, *Time*, and *Asiaweek.*

Country Reports
http://www.countryreports.org/
This site provides information on countries of the world.

Non-Christian World Religions/Belief Systems
http://www.refuge-outreach.org/religions/homepage.html
This site provides background information about religions found around the world.

U.S. Library of Congress Country Studies.
http://lcweb2.loc.gov/frd/cs/cshome.html
This site provides extensive history, geography, economic and other perspectives of Asian and other world countries.

The World Factbook
http://www.cia.gov/cia/publications/factbook/
This Central Intelligence Agency (CIA) site provides updated information about countries of the world.

Abortion, 16
Acupuncture, 23
Aerospace industry, 95
Agriculture
    China, 13, 22, 23, 25, 90, 92
    Japan, 13
    Korea, 13
    Mongolia, 98–99
AIDS, 60
Analects, 62–63
Arts, 65–67
    China, 29, 65–66
    Japan, 65, 66–67
    North Korea, 67
    and religion, 65, 67
    South Korea, 67
Asuka period, 32
Atmospheric hazards, 4–5, 15–17, 98
Atomic weapons. *See* Nuclear weapons

Baekje Kingdom, 25
Bak, Hyeokgeose, 25
Beijing, China, 29, 52
Britain
    and China, 30
    and Korea, 37–38
Buddha, 63–64
Buddhism
    and arts, 65, 67
    China, 25, 26, 65
    Japan, 32, 33, 64
    Korea, 36–37
    Mongolia, 64
    and Shinto, 61
    South Korea, 64
    Taiwan, 64
    Tibet, 65
Buildings, tallest, 92
Burma, and Japan, 46
Bushido (samurai code of living), 34

Calligraphy, 66, 67
Cantonese language, 59
Chang'an, China, 32
Chen, Shui-bian, 104, 108
Chiang, Kai-shek, 44, 51, 52, 73, 75

Children per woman, 59
China
    agriculture, 13, 22, 23, 25, 90, 92
    arts, 29, 65–66
    attacked by Japan, 29, 44
    and Britain, 30
    Buddhism, 25, 26, 65
    cities, 22, 26–27, 92, 96
    citizen rights and responsibilities,
        83–84, 85
    climate and ecosystems, 11, 13
    Confucianism, 23, 24, 26, 27,
        28, 63
    constitution, 74, 83, 85
    current history and status, 54
    early contact with Japan, 26
    early humans, 20–21
    earthquakes, 14–15, 18
    economy, 90, 92, 93, 94, 95–97, 103
    environmental issues, 6, 96–97
    flooding, 17
    foods, 67–68
    foreign relations, 85, 86
    future challenges, 105–106, 108
    government, 5, 71, 72, 73,
        75–76, 87
    gross domestic product, 93, 94, 95
    Han Dynasty, 23–25
    history, 21–31, 42–43, 51–52
    international trade, 30, 33, 86
    and Japan, 31–32, 34, 46, 75
    Jin Dynasty, 26
    and Korea, 25
    land, 8, 10–11, 97
    language, 59
    military power, 22–23, 27–28
    Ming Dynasty, 23, 29, 39
    Mongol era, 28
    and Mongolia, 38, 39, 43
    and North Korea, 50, 51
    population, 1, 58, 60, 105
    Qing Dynasty, 29–31, 42
    religion, 23–28, 61–63, 65
    Shang Dynasty, 22–23
    Song Dynasty, 26–28
    Sui Dynasty, 26

and Taiwan, 3, 4, 39, 72, 83, 108
Tang Dynasty, 26, 32
technology, 5, 23, 31
tourism, 24
and United States, 52, 75, 86
Xia Dynasty, 22
Yuan Dynasty, 28, 38, 39
Zhou Dynasty, 23, 62
Chinese Communist Party, 43–44,
    51–52, 72, 75
Chopsticks, 22, 68
Chosun Dynasty, 36–38
Christianity, 33, 34, 65
Cities
    China, 22, 26–27, 92, 96
    Japan, 34
Citizen rights and responsibilities,
    83–85
    China, 83–84, 85
    Japan, 85
    Mongolia, 85
    North Korea, 83, 84, 85
    South Korea, 85
    See also government
Civil service system, Chinese, 26
Climate and ecosystems, 5, 11, 13
"Comfort women" (prostitutes),
    46–47
Communes, 52
Communist Party (China), 43–44,
    51–52, 72, 75
Communist Party (Mongolia), 72
Confucianism
    China, 23, 24, 26, 27, 28, 63
    Japan, 27, 32, 34
    Korea, 27, 36, 37, 63
    Singapore, 63
    Taiwan, 63
Confucius, 62–63
Constitutions, 72–73, 74
    China, 74, 83, 85
    Japan, 74, 76–77
    Mongolia, 74, 85
    North Korea, 74, 78, 80, 84, 85
    South Korea, 74, 80–81
    Taiwan, 74, 82
    See also government

Consumerism, in China, 96
Currency, 94

Daimyo, 33–34
Dams, 17–18
Deflation, in Japan, 97
Deforestation, 17, 97
Demilitarized zone (DMZ), 51, 107
Democratic Progressive Party
    (Taiwan), 104–105
Deng, Xiaoping, 96
Deserts
    China, 8, 97
    climate and ecosystems, 10, 13
    Mongolia, 8
Diet (Japan's legislature), 44, 47, 77
Diseases, 60–61
DMZ (demilitarized zone), 51, 107
Drought, 5

Earthquakes, 4, 14–15, 18
East Asia
    countries included in, 3
    location, 4, 5, 8
    population, 4, 9
    size of region, 8
Economy, 88–103
    China, 90, 92, 93, 94, 95–97, 103
    East Asia and the global economy,
        102–103
    future challenges, 105–106
    industrial age, 89–90
    Japan, 88, 89–90, 93, 94, 97–98,
        103
    measures of economic
        development, 92–93, 94
    Mongolia, 4, 98–100, 103
    North Korea, 88, 92, 93, 94,
        100–101, 103
    regional contrasts, 90, 92
    South Korea, 4, 5, 101, 103
    Taiwan, 4, 5, 54, 102, 103
    See also Gross domestic product
        (GDP); International trade
Ecosystems and climate, 5, 11, 13
Edo, Japan, as capital of Japan, 33–34
    See also Tokyo, Japan

Edo period, 33–35
Eightfold Path, 64
Elevation and climate, 13
Environmental hazards, 14–17, 98
Environmental issues, 6, 86, 96–97
Erlitous, China, 22
Ethnic groups, 59
Europe
    and Mongolia, 38
    and Taiwan, 39
Everest, Mount, 10

Falungong, 52, 83–84
Flooding, 5, 16, 17
Food aid to North Korea, 92
Foods, 67–69
    China, 67–68
    Japan, 68
    Korea, 68
    Mongolia, 68
    Taiwan, 68
Foot binding, 60
Foreign relations, 71–72, 85–87
    China, 85, 86
    Japan, 85, 86
    Mongolia, 85, 86
    North Korea, 85–86
    South Korea, 85, 86
    Taiwan, 85, 86
    See also government
Formosa. See Taiwan
Formosa Strait, 72, 108
Four Modernizations, 96
Four Tigers, 101, 102
Fuji, Mount, 10, 14
Future challenges, 104–108
    China, 105–106, 108
    Japan, 106, 107
    North Korea, 106–108
    South Korea, 106–108
    Taiwan, 104–105, 106, 108

GDP. See Gross domestic product
    (GDP)
Genghis Khan, 28, 38
Geologic hazards, 4, 14–15, 98

Gobi Desert, 10
Goguryeo Kingdom, 25
Government, 71–87
    China, 5, 71, 72, 73, 75–76, 87
    citizen rights and responsibilities,
        83–85
    constitutions, 72–73, 74
    foreign relations, 71–72, 85–87
    Japan, 5, 71, 76–77, 87
    Mongolia, 5, 71, 72, 77–78, 87
    North Korea, 5, 71, 78–80
    South Korea, 5, 49, 71, 80–81, 87
    Taiwan, 5, 71, 72, 81–83, 87
Great Hural (Mongolia), 78
Great Wall of China, 23–24, 29
Gritzner, Charles F., 89–90
Gross domestic product (GDP)
    China, 93, 94, 95
    defined, 92–93
    Japan, 93, 94, 97
    Mongolia, 94, 100
    North Korea, 93, 94
    South Korea, 94, 101
    Taiwan, 94, 102
    See also economy
Guangdong Province, China, 60, 61

Hakka dialects, 59
Han Dynasty, 23–25
Hangul (Korean alphabet), 37
Hao, China, as capital of Zhou
    Dynasty, 23
Hazards
    atmospheric, 4–5, 15–17, 98
    geologic, 4, 14–15, 98
Heian, Japan, as capital of Japan, 32
    See also Kyoto, Japan
Heian period, 32
Himalayas, 5, 8, 10
Hirohito (emperor of Japan), 44, 47
Hiroshima, Japan, bombing, 47
History, 19–54
    China, 21–31, 42–43, 51–52
    early humans, 20–21
    Japan, 31–36, 43–48
    Korea, 25, 36–38, 48–51

Mongolia, 38–39, 43
Taiwan, 39
twenty-first century, 51–52
HIV/AIDS, 60
Hong Kong, ceded to British by
China, 30
Hongwu (emperor of China), 29
House of Councillors (Japan), 77
House of Representatives (Japan), 77
Huang (Yellow) River, China
early history, 21
flooding, 17
land features, 10–11
Humans, early, 20–21

Ieyasu, Tokugawa, 33–34
Inchon, South Korea, 49
Indochina, and Japan, 46
Indonesia, and Japan, 46
Industrial age, 89–90
Inner Mongolia, 39, 43, 47
    See also China; Mongolia
International trade
China, 30, 33, 86
East Asia, 5, 68–69, 86, 102, 106
Japan, 33, 34, 86, 98
Mongolia, 99–100
North Korea, 100–101
South Korea, 86, 101
Taiwan, 86, 102
    See also economy
Islam, 65
Isolation
and culture, 7–8
and foreign relations, 85–86
Italy, and Korea, 37–38

Japan
agriculture, 13
arts, 65, 66–67
Asuka period, 32
attacks China, 29, 44
Buddhism, 32, 33, 64
and China, 31–32, 34, 46, 75
Christianity, 33, 34
cities, 34

citizen rights and responsibilities, 85
climate and ecosystems, 11, 13
Confucianism, 27, 32, 34
constitution, 74, 76–77
current history and status, 54
customs, 55
early contact with China, 26
economy, 88, 89–90, 93, 94,
    97–98, 103
environmental hazards, 14, 98
environmental issues, 6
foods, 68
foreign relations, 85, 86
future challenges, 106, 107
geologic hazards, 14, 15
government, 5, 71, 76–77, 87
gross domestic product, 93, 94, 97
Heian period, 32
history, 31–36, 43–48
international trade, 33, 34, 86, 98
isolation and culture, 8
Kamakura period, 32–33
Kofun period, 32
and Korea, 31, 32, 36, 37–38, 46, 48
language, 59
military power, 35–36
and Mongolia, 33, 38, 46, 47
mountains, 10
Muromachi period, 32–33
Nara period, 32
nationalism, 33, 34–35, 36, 44
and Netherlands, 34
population, 9, 34, 58, 105
religion, 27, 32, 33, 34–35, 61, 64
and Ring of Fire, 9–10
and Russia, 36, 47
Shinto, 33, 34–35
and Taiwan, 31, 36, 39
technology, 5, 35
Tokugawa period, 33–35
and United States, 46, 47–48, 8
    6, 98
Japan Communist Party, 77
Japanese language, 59
Jiang, Zemin, 108
Jimmu (emperor of Japan), 31, 76

Jin Dynasty, 26
Judicial Yuan (Taiwan), 83

Kabuki (stylized theater), 67
Kamakura period, 32–33
Kami (sacred spirits), 61, 62
Karst topography, 10
Khalkha Mongol language, 59
Kim, Il Sung, 48, 49, 78
Kim, Jong Il, 72–73, 78, 80
KMT. *See* Kuomintang (KMT)
Kobe, Japan earthquakes, 15
Kofun period, 32
Koguryo Kingdom, 25
Kokkai (House of Councillors)
    (Japan), 77
Korea
    agriculture, 13
    Baekje Kingdom, 25
    and Britain, 37–38
    Buddhism, 36–37
    and China, 25
    Chosun Dynasty, 36–38
    climate and ecosystems, 11, 13
    Confucianism, 27, 36, 37, 63
    early humans, 21
    foods, 68
    history, 25, 36–38, 48–51
    isolation and culture, 8
    and Italy, 37–38
    and Japan, 31, 32, 36, 37–38, 46, 48
    Koguryo Kingdom, 25
    Koryo Dynasty, 36–37
    languages, 37, 48
    and Manchus, 37
    and Mongolia, 36, 38
    and Russia, 37–38, 48–49
    Shinto, 48
    Silla Kingdom, 25
    Unified Silla Kingdom, 25
    and United States, 37–38, 48–49
    See also North Korea; South Korea
Korean language, 59
Korean War, 49–51
Korean Workers Party, 80

Koryo Dynasty, 36–37
Kublai Khan, 28, 38
Kuomintang (KMT)
    Chiang Kai-shek as leader, 75
    history, 42, 43–44, 51–52
    presidential elections (2004),
        104–105
    and Taiwan, 73
Kyakhta, Treaty of, 43
Kyoto, Japan
    as capital of Japan, 32–33
    growth of, 34
Kyoto Protocol, 86
Kyushu, Japan tsunamis, 15

Labor force, 94
Land, 5, 8–11
Languages
    China, 59
    Japan, 59
    Korea, 37, 48
    Mongolia, 59
    North Korea, 59
    South Korea, 59
    Taiwan, 58, 59
Lao Tsu, 65
Law, rule of, 72, 73
Legislative Yuan (Taiwan), 82–83
Lien, Chan, 104
Life expectancy, 58, 59
Li River, China, 3–4
Literacy rate, 59, 60
Liu, Bang, 24
Location of East Asia region, 4, 5, 8
Loess deposits, 10
Long March, 75
Lu, Annette, 104

MacArthur, Douglas, 47, 49
Malaya, and Japan, 46
Male/female ratio, 59
Man, rule of, 72–73, 80
Manchukuo, 44, 46
Manchuria, 44, 47, 52

Manchus
    and Korea, 37
    and Mongolia, 39
    Qing Dynasty, 29–31
    and Taiwan, 39
Mandarin Chinese language, 58, 59
Mansfield, Mike, 105
Mao, Zedong, 52, 60, 73, 75
Meiji Restoration, 35–36
Middle path (Buddhism), 63
Military power
    China, 22–23, 27–28
    Japan, 35–36
    Mongolia, 38, 39
Ming Dynasty, 23, 29, 39
Mongol era, 28
Mongolia
    agriculture, 98–99
    and China, 38, 39, 43
    citizen rights and responsibilities, 85
    climate and ecosystems, 11, 13
    constitution, 74, 85
    current history and status, 54
    desert, 8
    economy, 4, 98–100, 103
    and Europe, 38
    foods, 68
    foreign relations, 85, 86
    government, 5, 71, 72, 77–78, 87
    gross domestic product, 94, 100
    history, 38–39, 43
    international trade, 99–100
    and Japan, 33, 38, 46, 47
    and Korea, 36, 38
    land, 10
    language, 59
    and Manchus, 39
    military power, 38, 39
    population, 1, 58, 60, 105
    religion, 64
    and Russia, 38, 39, 43, 100
Mongolian People's Revolutionary
    Party, 77
Montreal Protocol, 86
Mountains, 10, 14

Muromachi period, 32–33
Mutsuhito (emperor of Japan), 35, 36

Nagasaki, Japan bombing, 47
Nanjing, China, as capital of Ming
    Dynasty, 29
Nanjing, Treaty of, 30
Nanking (Nanjing) massacre, 44
Nara, Japan, as capital of Japan, 32
Nara period, 32
National Assembly (South Korea), 81
National Assembly (Taiwan), 83
Nationalism
    China, 42
    Japan, 33, 34–35, 36, 44
National People's Congress
    (China), 75
National People's Party (China). See
    Kuomintang (KMT)
Natural environment, 7–18
    atmospheric hazards, 4–5,
        15–17, 98
    climate and ecosystems, 11, 13
    flooding, 5, 16, 17
    geologic hazards, 4, 14–15, 98
    isolation and culture, 7–8
    the land, 8–11
    Three Gorges Dam, 17–18
Netherlands, and Japan, 34
Nikkei stock index, 97
Nirvana, 64
Nobunaga, Oda, 33
North Korea
    arts, 67
    and China, 50, 51
    citizen rights and responsibilities,
        83, 84, 85
    constitution, 74, 78, 80, 84, 85
    current history and status, 54
    economy, 88, 92, 93, 94,
        100–101, 103
    environmental issues, 6
    foreign relations, 85–86
    formation of, 48–49
    future challenges, 106–108

government, 5, 49, 71, 78–80
gross domestic product, 93, 94
international trade, 100–101
isolation, 70, 85–86
language, 59
nuclear weapons, 71–72, 86, 100,
    106–107
population, 58, 105
religion, 61, 63
and South Korea, 106–108
See also Korea; Korean War;
    South Korea
Nuclear weapons, 47, 51, 54
    North Korea, 71–72, 86, 100,
        106–107

Oil trade, 105, 106
Onjo (king of Korea), 25
Open Door policy (U.S.), 31
Opium, 30
Opium Wars, 30
Osaka, Japan
    earthquakes, 15
    growth of, 34
Outer Mongolia, 39, 42, 43
    See also Mongolia

Pacific Ocean
    access to international trade, 5
    as border, 4, 8
    tsunamis, 15
    See also Ring of Fire
Paintings, 66, 67
Pearl Harbor, Hawaii attack, 46
Peking Man, 20–21
People, 55–70
    arts, 65–67
    food, 67–69
    population, 58–61
    religion, 61–65
People's Liberation Party (China), 52
People's Republic of China. *See* China
Perry, Matthew C., 35
Petronas Towers, 92
Philippines, and Japan, 46
Plateau of Tibet, 8, 10, 13

Polo, Marco, 28, 68
Population, 58–61
    China, 1, 58, 60, 105
    East Asia, 4, 9
    Japan, 9, 34, 58, 105
    Mongolia, 1, 58, 60, 105
    North Korea, 58, 105
    South Korea, 58, 60, 105
    Taiwan, 58, 60, 105
    Tokyo, Japan, 34
P-Q-R-S-T model, 89–90, 101, 103
Prostitutes, 46–47
Purchasing power parity (PPP),
    93, 94

Qianglong (emperor of China), 29–30
Qin army, 24
Qing Dynasty, 29–31, 42

Religion, 61–65
    and arts, 65, 67
    China, 23–28, 61–63, 65
    Japan, 27, 32, 33, 34–35, 61, 64
    Mongolia, 64
    North Korea, 61, 63
    Shinto, 33, 34–35, 48, 61–62
    Singapore, 63
    South Korea, 63, 64
    Taiwan, 63, 64
    See also Buddhism; Christianity;
        Confucianism; Shinto
Republic of China, 73
    See also China; Taiwan
Republic of Korea. *See* South Korea
Rhee, Syngman, 49
Rice, 68
Ring of Fire, 9–10, 14
    See also Pacific Ocean
Robotics, 89
Rule of law, 72, 73
Rule of man, 72–73, 80
Russia
    and Japan, 36, 47
    and Korea, 37–38, 48–49
    and Mongolia, 38, 39, 43, 100
Russian Chinese language, 59
Russian language, 59

Samurai (warrior class), 34, 35
SARS (severe acute respiratory syndrome), 60–61
Sculpture, 65–66, 67
Sejong (king of Korea), 37
Self-Strengthening Movement, 31
Seoul, Korea, as capital of Korea, 37
Severe acute respiratory syndrome (SARS), 60–61
Sex ratio, 59
Shaanzi Province, China
earthquakes, 15
Shandong, China, 43
Shang Dynasty, 22–23
Shanghai, China, 92
Shanghainese language, 59
Shanghai World Financial Center, 92
Shang Zhou (king of Shang Dynasty), 23
Shinto
and Buddhism, 61
Japan, 33, 34–35
Korea, 48
Shoes, 55
Showa period, 44
Shugi-in (House of Representatives) (Japan), 77
Siddhartha Gautama, 63–64
Silk Road, 10, 25, 68
Silla Kingdom, 25, 36
Sinanthropus pekinensis (Peking Man), 20–21
Singapore
Confucianism, 63
and Japan, 46
Sino-Japanese War, 31, 36, 39
Sino-Soviet Treaty of Friendship, Alliance, and Mutual Assistance, 47
Size of East Asia region, 8
Skyscrapers, 92
Slippers, 55
Soils, 13
Song Dynasty, 26–28
South Korea
arts, 67
citizen rights and responsibilities, 85
constitution, 74, 80–81
current history and status, 54
economy, 4, 5, 101, 103
environmental issues, 6
foreign relations, 85, 86
formation of, 48–49
future challenges, 106–108
government, 5, 49, 71, 80–81, 87
gross domestic product, 94, 101
international trade, 86, 101
language, 59
and North Korea, 106–108
population, 58, 60, 105
religion, 63, 64
technology, 5
typhoons, 15
and United States, 50, 51, 86
See also Korea; Korean War; North Korea
Soviet Union. See Russia
Sui Dynasty, 26
Sun, Yat-sen, 42, 43, 73, 75
Sun Goddess, 31, 61
Supreme Court (Japan), 77
Supreme Court (Mongolia), 78
Supreme Court (South Korea), 81
Supreme People's Assembly (Korea), 80

Taipei 101 building, 92
Taiwan
and China, 3, 4, 39, 72, 83, 108
climate and ecosystems, 11, 13
constitution, 74, 82
current history and status, 54
economy, 4, 5, 54, 102, 103
environmental issues, 6
and Europe, 39
foods, 68
foreign relations, 85, 86
future challenges, 104–105, 106, 108
geologic hazards, 14
government, 5, 71, 72, 81–83, 87
gross domestic product, 94, 102
history, 39
international trade, 86, 102

and Japan, 31, 36, 39
languages, 58, 59
and Manchus, 39
population, 58, 60, 105
presidential elections,
    104–105, 108
religion, 63, 64
and Ring of Fire, 9
Taywan Kingdom, 39
technology, 5
Taiwanese language, 59
Taiwan Strait, 72, 108
Taklimakan (Takla Makan)
    Desert, 10
Tang Dynasty, 26, 32
Tangshan, China earthquakes, 14–15
Taoism, 23, 65
Taywan Kingdom, 39
Technology, 5–6
    China, 5, 23, 31
    Japan, 5, 35
    South Korea, 5
    Taiwan, 5
38th parallel, 49, 51
Three Gorges Dam, China, 17–18, 96
Three Kingdoms era, 25, 36
Three Principles of the People, 42, 73
Tiananmen Square demonstrations,
    52, 83
Tibet, Buddhism in, 65
Tibet, Plateau of, 8, 10, 13
Tokugawa period, 33–35
Tokyo, Japan
    earthquakes, 15
    population, 34
Tourism
    Great Wall of China, 24
    Li River, China, 3–4
Treaty of Kyakhta, 43
Treaty of Nanjing, 30
Tsunamis, 14, 15
Tsuyoshi, Inukai, 44

Turkic language, 59
Typhoons, 4–5, 15–16

Unemployment rates, 94
Unified Silla Kingdom, 25
United Nations, 49–50, 85, 86
United Nations Security Council, 85
United States
    and China, 52, 75, 86
    and Japan, 46, 47–48, 86, 98
    and Korea, 37–38, 48–49
    Open Door policy, 31
    and South Korea, 50, 51, 86
Urbanization. See Cities

Vegetation, 13
Volcanic activity, 14

Walls around cities, 22
Weather. See Climate and ecosystems
Women, status of, 60
World War I, 43, 44
World War II, 46–47, 75
Writing, 22, 66, 67
Wu Ti, 24

Xia Dynasty, 22
Xian, China, 65–66

Yang, Liwei, 95
Yangtze River, China, 17
    See also Three Gorges Dam
Yanshi, China, 22
Yellow River. See Huang (Yellow)
    River, China
Yellow Sea, 11
Yi, Song-gye, 36–37
Yokohama, Japan earthquakes, 15
Yuan, Shikai, 42–43
Yuan Dynasty, 28, 38, 39

Zhou Dynasty, 23, 62
Zhoukoudian, China, 20–21

page:

2:   © Mapping Specialists, Ltd.
3:   New Millennium Images
11: KRT/New Millennium Images
12: © Mapping Specialists, Ltd.
16: Associated Press, AP
20: Associated Press, AP
24: New Millennium Images
27: New Millennium Images
45: Associated Press, AP
50: Associated Press, AP
53: Associated Press, AP
56: New Millennium Images
57: © Mapping Specialists, Ltd.
64: New Millennium Images
66: KRT/New Millennium Images

69: New Millennium Images
76: Kyodo News/New Millennium Images
79: Kyodo News/New Millennium Images
82: Eye Press/New Millennium Images
84: Associated Press, AP
90: Kyodo News/New Millennium Images
91: © Mapping Specialists, Ltd.
95: KRT/New Millennium Images
99: New Millennium Images
107: KRT/New Millennium Images
Cover: New Millennium Images

DOUGLAS A. PHILLIPS is a lifetime educator, writer, and consultant who has worked and traveled in more than 85 countries on six continents. During his career, he has worked as a middle school teacher, a curriculum developer, an author, and a trainer of educators in many countries around the world. He has served as the President of the National Council for Geographic Education and has received the Outstanding Service Award from the National Council for the Social Studies, along with numerous other awards. He, his wife, and his two sons now reside in Arizona—a daughter is in Texas—where he writes and serves as a Senior Consultant for the Center for Civic Education. He has traveled to all of the countries in East Asia, with the exception of North Vietnam, and understands the importance of this region to the world today.

CHARLES F. ("FRITZ") GRITZNER is Distinguished Professor of Geography at South Dakota University in Brookings. He is now in his fifth decade of college teaching and research. During his career, he has taught more than 60 different courses, spanning the fields of physical, cultural, and regional geography. In addition to his teaching, he enjoys writing, working with teachers, and sharing his love for geography with students. As consulting editor for the MODERN WORLD NATIONS series, he has a wonderful opportunity to combine each of these "hobbies." Fritz has served as both President and Executive Director of the National Council for Geographic Education and has received the Council's highest honor, the George J. Miller Award for Distinguished Service. In March 2004, he won the Distinguished Teaching award from the American Association of Geographers at their annual meeting held in Philadelphia.